TRAPPED BY ISLAM

by
Barbara Dorsi

Copyright 2008 Barbara Dorsi

All rights reserved

No part of this book may be reproduced stored in a retrieval system or transmitted by any means electronic, mechanical, photocopying, recording or otherwise without written permission from the author.

ISBN:-
978-0-9559794-0-8
www.lulu.com

ACKNOWLEDGEMENTS

The book that you are about to read is the result of great support from my family, friends and all the lovely people around me. Everyone has contributed to changing the ways in which my information was gathered and I would like to say thank you very much to each and everyone who made this book become possible.

I would particularly like to thank, my mother, my brother, my sister, my dear friend Anita, Kiki, Stathis and of course the wonderful Nicola. I also want to acknowledge all the other people who cannot be named for reasons of confidentiality. You all know who you are, good luck and love you very much.

Barbara Dorsi was born in Athens, Greece in 1977, to a Greek Orthodox mother and a Libyan Muslim father, with one brother and later one sister.

She grew up and educated in Melissia in Athens in a tumultuous family life due to the poor relationship between her parents. In 1990 she moved to the north east of England, with her family where her father attempted to convert the family to Islam after finding religion again due to the large Islamic society that exists in the north east. The relationship between her parents and the family started to deteriorate considerably to the point where in 1996 they separated but things did not end there. Barbara is now a serving police officer and lives just outside London.

Forsaken by love

Betrayed by faith

Isolated by culture

CONTENTS

Monday -   Love is a powerful word
Tuesday -   She wasn't good enough for him
Wednesday -   Invasion or a Plague
Thursday -   Stacks of paper
Friday -   The facts
Saturday -   The camels back
Sunday -   The move

MONDAY

----Love is a Powerful Word----

Hestia curled up into the soft white leather armchair, as the door slammed, echoing through the house. She watched Zak walk out of her life for what seemed to be the thousandth time. Tears and more tears rolled down her face one by one, dripping onto her blue silk blouse that soaked them up like the sands of the Sahara where she and Zak had honeymooned.

Her heart pounded so hard, she didn't notice Hope creep back upstairs, leaving her to wallow in her misery and self-pity.

Out of the two emotions, self pity reigned highest as it always did, after an argument with Zak. It was as though they had a set routine to their arguments. After the initial eruption, Zak, would storm out of the house, leaving devastation in his wake.

Hurt, broken promises, bruised egos, painful memories and smashed possessions were all that remained. All of which paled into insignificance to the wounds he inflicted on her body. Physically and emotionally. Where had that wonderful gentleman gone, the one who vowed to love and protect her from a harsh world? But now, who could protect her from him?

His good looks and his ambition had slowly faded through the years, only to be replaced by frustration anger and bitterness. His thick wavy black hair was now peppered with grey. Wrinkles lined his still handsome face with thick, long, black eyelashes and finely shaped eyebrows. This pricked his vanity even more. He was a wry self-confident forty nine-year old, with eyes that always refused to trust. Zak spoke with a clipped accent that sounded very Greek, but still, after all these years speaking the Greek language, there were one or two words he didn't get quite right.

Zak had always felt under-valued by his wife and children. He always felt as if he was rejected, which hurt him to the core. He often described to friends and family that he was unheard and misunderstood by everyone, but they all knew these accusations were unfounded and that he never made any effort to correct his ways or even apologise to his family for his actions.

He had a very active imagination to the point of paranoia, which led to frequent arguments.

This one, like all the others, had started out with

something so small: the evening meal.

If Zak wanted an argument, he would pick on anything just so he could have one. He would not turn around and walk away. However this time, Hestia was ready for him. She knew it had been brewing for weeks.

With all the unexplained disappearances, the late nights and the lack of money, there was definitely something going on and she demanded an answer.

Was there another woman? Was he really feeling neglected? Was it Hestia's fault? Hestia often wondered.

"Hello Zak!"

"Hi!"

"How are you today?"

"Not bad…" That was his answer for everything.

"Are you hungry? Shall I set the table?"

"What's for dinner?"

Her eyes lit up as she smiled. "Fish and chips."

"Fish and chips? You must be kidding. Since when did you become English? I don't like fish and fucking chips! You know I don't eat that crap! Don't walk away when I am talking to you! Hestia, I'm talking to you!."

"I'm not interested, Zak. I'm in no mood to argue with you, so please don't start…"

Hestia hesitated while biting her bottom lip, hoping he wouldn't start an argument.

"Don't start? Don't start? What do you mean don't fucking start?" He stepped closer to the kitchen, towards Hestia as his voice raised. "I've been out all day, trying to sort things out for the shop and I come home for a decent meal, to find out that you've prepared fish and chips? How on earth…"

"Zak, stop! Now! The children are upstairs and I don't want to argue where they are…"

"Maybe I do you stupid bitch! So, what are you going to do about it? Eh? What are you going to do about it?"

"Zak, please…I'm begging you Zak."

"I've had enough of you!"

"What? You've had enough of us? Well, let me tell you something, Zak. I've had enough of your late nights, you sleeping around, your moods, not coming home at all. Where were you last night, Zak? What have you been up to? What's going on?"

"Don't be so bloody stupid! Who are *you* to ask *me* questions? I am a man and in the name of Allah I can go wherever I want, whenever I want and I can be with whoever I want!"

"I'm your wife, Zak, in case you forgotten who I am. I have every right to know where you've been and I'm sick of your pathetic lies, your dis…"

The resounding slap cut off the rest of her sentence. As he walked away, she was left staring at his back.

The sound of the footsteps on the stairs broke her reverie as her maternal instincts surfaced. She could not let her three children see her like this.

So, she stood, then went to the kitchen to wash her face with cold water, hoping to hide her emotional scars, but more importantly her physical ones.

Thankfully this time it was only a slap, and not the blunt hits she had to lie to her children about and hide from friends and family until the redness, bruises and cuts had healed.

Hope was first through the door. "Has he gone

mummy?"

"Who?"

Hope looked at her mum, laughed and said "Daddy, who else?"

"Sorry love, I was miles away. Uh, yes he has."

"Will dad be coming back?"

"Maybe…later…maybe…."

Hestia lied, knowing full well he would not return for days and, when he did, he would be full of promises that he wouldn't and couldn't ever keep.

Hope was drawn by the comforting sound of her favourite programme on TV. Her daughter, Athena had most likely turned on the TV, knowing how easily upset Hope could get and how her emotional problems had lately been leading to physical ones, mainly a loss of appetite.

Lately, everyone had commented on Hope's loss of appetite and loss of weight. Her teachers especially were concerned about the increasing time she was spending in the girls' toilets.

This embarrassed Hope even further, as it was often mentioned in front of the class.

Hestia knew this was becoming a problem, but the doctors blamed the stress on having a disruptive life, which Hestia tried to avoid at all costs.

After about half an hour, Hope was totally absorbed in the magical life of Sabrina the Teenage Witch, so Athena sneaked away to the kitchen to speak and comfort her mum.

"Are you okay, Mum?"

"Yes…" Hestia replied, as a tear rolled down her cheek.

"Do you want me to do anything mum?"

"No….just put the kettle on…" Hestia murmured.

Athena put her arms round her mum telling her everything would be okay.

Athena was about 5'5', with soft, dark, curly hair usually up in a ponytail. She hardly ever wore any make-up and her favourite clothes were black jeans and black tops. She worked hard everyday, trying to make things easier for Hestia. She was Hestia's second youngest daughter. In her late teens and full of life, she always put her mother first.

On numerous occasions, Hestia tried to tell Athena to go out with her friends, just so that she could get out of the house and do something she would enjoy, but she always found an excuse to stay in and look after her mum and her younger sister.

The sound of the phone made both of them jump and stare.

Hestia moved first and checked the caller ID, which stated *unavailable* and hesitantly, answered it.

"Hello?!"

"Hestia? Is that you?"

"Oh…hi, Dora. How…are…"

"Hestia? I didn't recognise your voice. You are very… quiet. What's wrong?"

Hestia could not hold back the tears and said in a trembling voice "All I want is for Zak to love me the way I love him…and…"

"Is he there, Hestia?"

"No. He's gone and I doubt if he'll be back tonight."

"Oh love, I wish I could be there to try and sort a few things out."

"It's the same thing happening all the time. We used to argue once a year, then it became once every six months. Now it's once a fortnight and soon it'll be every day."

"Listen to me, Hestia. Pack your bags, take the kids and come to stay with us in Greece. You should have never moved to Middlesbrough. After all who have you got there? You have no friends and no family, he has his Muslim friends and he now wants all of you to become Muslims. You manage to get yourself half way up and then he puts you half way down again."

"Things are not as easy as they seem Dora. I wish they were…but…"

"You just cannot live your life in fear."

"I know… but leaving all together is not the answer"

"What is the answer then? Leave him! Leave Zak, Hestia"

"What about the kids, Dora?"

"Hestia, the children will be better off without all the arguments. Without…"

"I know… it's easy to say, but…"

"Where are the kids now?"

"Hope is watching TV, Athena is with me and Troy is in his bedroom getting ready to go out!"

"Just pack your bags and come back to Greece!"

"Oh Dora! I'll try and sort something out today. I'm gonna have to phone him later and speak to him."

"So what will you do? What will you say to him?"

"I'll phone him in the shop tonight because I've got to sort it out."

"Okay love. Let me know."

"I will Dora. I'll phone you tomorrow."

Hestia put the phone down and joined Athena at the dining table where she had made a cup of tea and some biscuits.

But Hestia didn't feel hungry. She had lost her appetite. Within minutes, Hestia was lost in her own little world. She stared out of the window and her eyes seemed to sink deeper into her brain.

Athena tried to make conversation, but when she looked at her mum she knew she was miles away.

Hestia felt as if she was waiting for some kind of

healing to begin. She often remembered of all the years that had been forgotten and wondered if pain ever went away or became buried within one's heart when one passed away.

All of a sudden, Hestia whispered, "Never say *I love you*, if you don't mean it. *I love you* are powerful words and if you say it, just for the sake of it, it's a throw away promise and it means a little bit less every time you mention it."

"What was all that about, Mum?"

"Just take my advice, Athena. Just take my advice, you will understand one day."

Troy, her eldest son, ran down the stairs, put his arms round his mum and kissed her. For a second, Hestia seemed frightened but soon realised who he was.

Troy was six foot tall, with short dark hair, big brown eyes with long eyelashes and always clean shaved. With gel in hair and his clothes always in fashion, his upbeat well groomed fashion conscious exterior was not a true reflection of his inner self; inwardly he didn't care about keeping in step with others. He hardly ever showed emotions or feelings even though he felt them; sometimes even more than anyone else.

"I won't be too long tonight, Mum I 'am going because the lads are waiting outside for me."

"Okay Troy. Bye," said Hestia to her son as he hurried out the door, leaving a scented trail of after-shave in his wake.

"Mum!" Hope shouted from the lounge.

Athena smiled wryly and went to see what Hope wanted, leaving Hestia time to escape to the sanctuary of her back garden.

This was Hestia's favourite place of the house. Here no one disturbed her; it was an unwritten rule.

Once she was out there, everyone else found something else to do. She spent the next few hours, weeding, watering and dead heading as she wandered through the garden. Hestia loved all of her flowers, but her favourite were roses that grew in profusion along the house wall. It wasn't the vivid colours she liked most, but the scent that seemed to permeate the air and follow a person, around especially at this time of the evening. These were her friends.

Friends that always listened. Listened without

judging or criticising her situation.

All too soon, she had to leave her little Eden if only to put Hope to bed. Tonight would be even more tiring than usual, as Hope was bound to talk about her father's behaviour.

Hope co-operated and flew though her nightly rituals, which usually took at least half an hour. Once she was tucked up in bed, she asked her question.

"Mummy, when will daddy come back?"

If only Hope was older. Hestia took a deep breath and a step forward before answering, knowing that she would have to re-assure her five- year- old- daughter. She crossed her fingers as she said,: "He won't be too long, love. He has a few jobs to do and then he'll be back. You'll probably be asleep then but, he'll soon be back."

Hope didn't look convinced, but she settled down to her pillows.

As Hestia got ready to go, Hope asked;

"Will you be here in the morning, Mummy?"

"Of course I will, sweetheart! Why wouldn't I?" Hestia replied softly.

"I don't know, I'm just asking?"

"I'll always be here, sweetness. Daddy comes and goes, but I'll always be by your side, okay?" Hestia replied, trying to re assure Hope, but not to sound too intense.

"Okay," Hope whispered, as her enormous brown eyes brimmed with tears that she tried not to show.

Mother and daughter held onto each other so tight that neither one of them wanted to let go, but as Hope drifted to sleep, Hestia knew she had that call to make and it would take all her energy and concentration.

By 9.15 p.m., after leaving Athena to baby-sit Hope, Hestia felt strong enough to face Zak again.

Pulling up outside the shop, she walked quickly inside on shaky legs, passed the counter and into the kitchen where everything was being prepared, ready to confront Zak about his behaviour.

The only person there was John, an employee whom she got on with, but thought a little strange. He was about forty years old but looked much older, with hair that could not decide whether it was black or brown but definitely thinning on top. He had a clawed right hand and over the many years since the accident that damaged it, had mastered ingenious ways of using it to its full potential. The accident also gave him a profound limp in his right leg and sometimes when the light was dim at the back of the shop, he lurched around like Egor as he collected more pizza bases from the freezer. Hestia didn't mind any of the physical conditions or use them to form her opinion of him. It was his sly, greedy nature that disturbed her. She knew he was on the 'take' but could never prove it. He was a good worker and general dogs body so they kept him employed.

"Hi John! Where's Zak?" she asked surprised at not seeing Zak sulking in the back.

"You have just missed him. He came earlier, but he said he was busy and left about 8.15" he replied with a smile.

Like all people, John had a soft spot for such a kind and patient woman as Hestia.

"I forgot to give him the phone bill though," John said as he handed it to her. "Could you ask him to sort it out? Only we have had a call to say it's well overdue and they are threatening to cut us off. If that happens, we won't be able to do deliveries and that's most of our business."

"Really?" said Hestia, unable to mask her amazement. Zak was not usually so careless where making money was concerned. "I'll make sure he'll sort it out." she promised with a smile, glancing at the unopened letter. "Isn't he coming back to close the shop then?"

"No, he asked me to do it. We are never busy on Mondays anyway." he assured, trying to ease her mind.

She frowned at the obvious reference that John wouldn't be seeing him tonight.

"Oh well, in that case, I'll take this with me." She raised the letter slightly. "See you later John. If you need anything, let me know." She knew the effort that was required to run the shop and by rights it should not fall on John.

"I'm fine, Hestia. You go and relax. Like I said, it is always quiet on Mondays. See you later."

Hestia got as far as the next street before parking the car and opening the letter. She scanned the letter, noting the multitude of numbers detailed there, but two stood out amongst the others. Both were in Libya. The first of the two was the phone number for his oldest sister house, Jemima. The other number was unknown to Hestia. This was the number that made up the bulk of the £319.46 phone bill.

Puzzled and apprehensive, Hestia made her way back home, unsure if she should share her suspicions with her daughter. But one look at the frown on Athena's face made up her mind; she would not add to her daughter's troubles, while thoughts still disturbed her about whom Zak had spent hundreds of pounds speaking to.

The fact that it wasn't family was certain. But whether it was male or female was less so.

TUESDAY

*---She Wasn't Good Enough
For Him---*

Hestia lay awake and looked at the clock again, then sighed. It annoyed her that he still had the power to disturb her, even when he was not there.

She turned and lay on her back to stare at the boring pale cream and peach round lampshade, which she knew every inch of. Then she closed her eyes, once again, and made a conscious effort to relax and sleep, but she failed miserably.

Three more hours and Hope would wake up, get into her mum's bed and then proceed to talk about everything possible and everything else that was impossible, most of which would start with the dreaded word, "Why?"

Still knowing the children would notice the dark circles underneath her eyes, Hestia tried to block out the thoughts that refused to let her find peace in sleep.

The warm bath full of bubbles, prepared by Athena, and a mug of hot chocolate had relaxed her body considerably, but that was almost six hours ago. Now she was tossing and turning, considering whether or not to straighten the rumpled sheets.

There was a time when she would have welcomed rumpled sheets and their cause, but that was months ago, which now seemed like years.

Not that it was the actual sex that she missed, but more the intimacy, the closeness, and the feelings.

No matter what else he had deemed unfit and unacceptable, sex had never been a problem. Zak would always reach out to her in the dark and pull her close and hold her and love her, until she forgave him.

He knew her weakness and used it: love. Her love for him. Not just in the carnal way, but the fact that she wanted everything possible for him; work, friends, social life, nice house, meals always on the table, good kids, even the religion.

When they made their big move to England to be with Athena and Troy who were attending schools and colleges, they brought their whole life in cases, boxes, and even one or two crates.

Hestia was expecting to start a new life, a new beginning in her husband's arms and her children's future, but no sooner had they settled in with Zak's brother, Mustafa and his wife, Hamida, then he found religion with little help from his two younger brothers, Mustafa and Haled who were fanatic about their religion.

This didn't bother Hestia much to begin with. In fact, she thought that it was good for Zak to spend time with his family. The fact that Zak wasn't Greek Orthodox any more didn't matter, as Hestia always believed in the right to choose one's religion. England, being the free-thinking country it was, she knew being a Muslim was not the problem it was in Greece. Up until recently, Muslims were not welcomed or suffered lightly in Greece; their history was too recent and not yet forgotten. But as the months passed, things changed. Small things, such as spending time with other Muslims and being invited to their houses, so often that Hestia realised that she did not have one friend that was not a Muslim.

They were all really nice people; most of the women were English that had married Muslim men and had converted which was very unusual to see. Sometimes it felt as if they had moved to Libya or another Arab country and not England with so many Muslims around.

This still didn't bother Hestia, up until the children got involved. Then, suddenly everything changed. Zak was now everyone's leader. Where once they were a family, now they were alone and separate. Where once he was the head of the family, he had now become the whole of the family. Everything had to be decided by him. No one was allowed to ever have an opinion that was considered to be anti-Muslim or pro-Christian. These things were punishable with violence.

Hestia felt puzzled and didn't know which way to turn. She couldn't understand what was happening to her family. Religion couldn't be the cause of all this devastation. Religion should be a positive force that brought people together and continued to bind them to each other through mutual respect and trust, as though the whole community had been joined by marriage. This however seemed more like a divorce. It was as though her past and future had been separated permanently. Gone was the carefree life of Athens, in its place there was obedience and submission. Gone was the trust and unrestrained love, to be replaced by suspicion and violent rages. Gone were the friends and the ambition, until all that was left was his twisted interpretation of Koran!

Then came the removal of all the things that made their lives their own.

The main cause of distress was the changing of the children's names. From the moment the plane landed at Heathrow, Zak declared that his children would be known only by their Muslim names and, as they were to stay with his brothers family, Hamida, Mustafa and their two children—who were all Muslims, Hestia agreed if only to keep the peace.

She was familiar with this practise as Zak's family often visited their home in Greece and they all saw it at the time as a funny game they had to play for the short time their strange relatives stayed.

Although Troy readily answered to the name Osama, Athena often pretended not to hear her aunties and uncles when they called out Nadia, until her father gave her the look that meant trouble. They all knew that look. His look had the power to strike fear into their little hearts making them realise how close to the edge of violence he really was.

Being in England made Troy and Athena realise that what they once thought of as a funny game was actually deadly serious now.

No one called them Troy and Athena any longer other than their mother and that was only in private where no one else could hear them.

That was until they started attending their local school. It was there that they found themselves again. They rediscovered the freedom to just be themselves without having to be someone they did not want to be. Here they were simply kids amongst other kids doing everything that every other kid was allowed to do.

Even though Troy and Athena were Greek kids in an English school, with a very limited vocabulary, they felt able to fit in as they were not the only ones from a different cultural background. This was the one place their father had no control over their names, behaviour or opinions.

For any other children, school would feel like a chore that had to be endured. But for Troy and Athena, it felt like heaven. After a lifetime of relative freedom, for them to be subjected to six weeks of intense cultural changes with strict instruction in what to say, what to do and what to think, this sudden and complete liberation felt like awakening from a nightmare. But whilst they knew that nightmare would continue once they were back within their father's sphere, they relished their short time away from him.

During their first few weeks of school, the children's grasp of the English language improved dramatically. Where once they chose to speak Greek to each other, they now desperately tried to pick up every nuance of English, especially the slang words. This invariably caused problems at home. After telling his children several times that if they wanted to speak English, they were not to use words that were questionable. He finally snapped one day at tea time.

"This is bloody stupid, I told you that I want you to speak proper English, when I'm around. If you want to say something else, you say it in plain Greek. Am I understood?"

"But...dad... this is how we can practice and..."

"Practice? Practice? If you want to fucking practice, you practice at school, not yapping using foreign languages."

Athena couldn't keep quiet, so she joined in on the discussion. "For your information this is slang. It's English, if you didn't already know and…"

"Look at you, I think your mother should be proud to have children like you, having no respect towards your father. Your mum taught you well."

"Leave mum out of this. I'm old enough to have an opinion and say what I want to say," said Athena.

"Just go to your bedrooms, kids. It's not worth having an argument at the moment. Come on! Go! And finish off your homework!"

Hestia felt the need to interfere before things got out of hand and certainly before Zak got violent with them.

"Just look at them, Hestia. They show no respect. They treat me like shit and you have the cheek to sit there and listen to them arguing with me! Times like these you should stick up for me and tell them to shut their mouth"

"This is nonsense, Zak. The kids respect you. They listen to everything you say. They do what you tell them to do. Look at other kids their age and…"

"…and what, Hestia? Compare? It's all your fault. They don't even use their names in front of the family, let alone anything else. And you encourage them to use the stupid Greek names, despite…"

"How dare you, Zak? We both decided to christen the children. We both decided to give them those names and now you are telling me this is my fault? I can't understand what's happening to us. You have become totally unreasonable…"

"Is that right? Putting the blame on me now? Yes that's right. You are an angel and so are your kids…Just look at you, you re a shit mother, a shit wife, you have shit children...just admit it."

"Our kids Zak, our kids!"

"If I had my way, they would not be disrespectful and full of attitude…they would be good Muslims. Athena would have a hijab, dress like a nice Muslim girl, you should be dressed like a muslim wife and do what you re told. I am working on it."

"Just listen to yourself, Zak!" Hestia got up and went to the kitchen sink to do the washing up. Zak followed Hestia and whispered in her right ear "…you are nothing, you re ugly, lonely, incapable, miserable old woman. You should be happy and grateful for having me in your life. Without me you 're nothing Hestia. Just remember that". Within minutes, the front door slammed and Hestia knew Zak was storming out once again. It was as if he was trying to erase their whole identities and create them again in an image he thought suitably fit for a Muslim father to be proud of.

This was the main sticking point in the arguments that escalated after that decree. Hestia knew him so well. She knew she couldn't change his mind once he had made it up, so she tried to find a way round it, by avoiding calling them by name.

She often wondered if that was the right thing to do.

Whenever there were visitors around, Hestia would whisper their names: Hope, Athena and Troy and if Zak would have heard it, it meant a night full of moods, black looks and eventually an argument.

It was like the whole family was acting for a religious film! This had a great effect on the children themselves; they refused to call each other by name because they didn't want to create more trouble for their mother. They had seen plenty of arguments and they would try to avoid them at all times.

Although that was the biggest problem, he continued to manipulate the family and create smaller problems that were equally as vicious.

Like the time when eight people were living in the same household and everyone's sanity was threatened every time there was the first bit of good news the whole family needed to agree on.

Athena and Troy arrived back at Hamida's and Mustafa's house to find their mother with packed suitcases. At first they both thought, "god she is going to leave him!" Then, she explained that the council had granted them a house. That night was to be their last with Hamida, Mustafa and the kids, and all the bad feelings that had gradually been developed over the last months. Now they would finally all have the personal space they needed. It proved to be one of the few genuine happy memories that Hestia could remember whilst living with Zak's brother and sister-in-law.

Hamida and Hestia spent hours in the kitchen, cooking everyone's favourite foods. The children laughed and giggled as they collected their personal belongings together and haphazardly stuffed them into bags uncaring in their excitement. Zak and Mustafa sat in state on the sofa watching the activity and smiling like some benevolent Santa Claus as if Zak had bestowed a great gift upon them.

A council house on a notorious estate meant barely anything, but even this was an improvement on not having a house at all. So with celebratory atmosphere, they all ate talked and joked and made merry. Then, after all was cleared away, and Hamida and Mustafa thanked Hestia and Zak, they went to bed with actual hope in their heads.

The next morning, when Hestia walked into the empty vandalised house, reality kicked in and, for all of ten minutes, she felt overwhelmed. Very soon she realised that the children had already decided on their rooms and were well on their way to dragging out everything that had been left by the last tenants. Well, she thought to herself, if my children can do this then, so can I! And with that thought in her head and the children's excited voices echoing through the empty rooms, Hestia took a deep breath and began to make that devastation into a home, for her troubled family. If this was to be a new start, then it would be the best new start she could make.

Over the next few months, a routine of sorts was established. Zak bought a shop close to the town centre and set it all up to sell pizzas and kebabs take away. He worked long hours, until three in the morning, then came home and slept 'until noon.

Hestia didn't like this as it resulted in having very little time together, but she admired him because he was working hard in order to build up his business and provide for his family.

The children went to school and studied hard, which was drummed into them at an early age; that if they wanted to live well then they must earn money. In order to earn money, they needed a good job and this could only be achieved by gaining good grades.

Troy and Athena came home from school about 3:30 in the afternoon and sat to have tea with their parents. This was the only time they spent any length of time with their father as he left for the shop at about 4:30 in the afternoon. They tried their hardest not to be annoying or offensive, and succeeded most of the time.

Hestia worked in the shop alongside Zak most nights, especially at weekends. But after one nasty argument about Hestia smiling to the male customers, she declared that she would not work there with him again. So with no job and no husband, and, except for a couple of hours in the afternoon, no children all day, Hestia felt restless and bored. She missed her family and friends back in Athens and often regretted living in the UK. But now, she had made her bed and would have to lay in it. So with her usual determination and pride, she put all her efforts and energy into her home and family and, if the only thing that was left to her was pride, she would use it to her advantage.

As November came to a close, the children's thoughts turned inevitable to the joy of Christmas. This was their favourite time of the year. They no longer were babies believing in Santa, but this didn't lessen their anticipation and excitement.

This year was to be a very upsetting year, though, as the children were not allowed to celebrate Christmas with the rest of the world. Zak's decision was non-negotiable.

Christmas had always been a time for celebrations, fun, happiness, presents, forgiveness and Father Christmas coming down through the chimney to drop all the pretty boxes under the tree. Christmas was always a momentous occasion in Greece and Zak always participated in the fun. He would always take his young children to the town, in Marousi, to a place called *Paradise Trees*, let them pick a tree and Hestia could guarantee that it would always be as tall as him.

At about 6 feet tall, Zak would then carry the tree home, surprise Hestia and they would spend hours decorating the tree with colourful bobbles, unusual lights, and then hang up the holly. He would stay up late with Hestia to wrap all the presents and hide them underneath the tree. It was always a time to gather the entire family and friends together in their beautiful and spacious house, have a drink, then wish everyone a very merry Christmas, all of which Zak participated in, until they moved to England.

All this lead to Troy and Athena being confused, worried, uncertain of their future and unable to have an opinion of their own.

Hestia, however, always found excuses for his behaviour and tried to co-operate. She knew in her heart that he needed her, but the need to control was stronger.

Control over the money. Control over the kids. Control over where she could go. Control of whom she could talk to. Control over what she could do. Control of what she could wear. He had become a control freak! This was a growing list that he added to daily depending on his irrational thoughts and actions.

Hestia tried to rationalise his behaviour all the time. She knew he hated being in the take-away shop he had and that he wanted to give up his business and find employment elsewhere. He wanted something he wouldn't have to worry about all the time, but his attitude would always be, "*Who would employ a man of my age?*" This could leave him being unemployed, he said, which would make things even harder and his moods even worse.

The businesses he tried to set up, he lost interest in and neglected. Leaving him feeling inadequate, ashamed and bad tempered, which he took out on her.

These things she could understand and forgive but the lies, the deceit, the affairs and drugs she could no longer ignore. These were the things she knew, without a doubt, would end her marriage.

She never let him see her cry; she never wanted to tell him how lonely she felt. She sometimes wanted room to breathe, time to think, but he never gave her the space she needed. One look in her eyes would tell him all he needed to know, but he never paid any attention to his own family and certainly not his wife.

She was good enough not to ask him when he'd be back. She was good enough to look after his family and his friends. She was good enough to prepare dinner. She was good enough to hoover and she was good enough to lie for him.

She often thought to her herself that *she wasn't good enough for him.* People change and maybe Zak will change too, she thought – one day.

The sound of the toilet flushing ended her

reverie. Hope was awake. She climbed in beside Hestia and put her cold feet against her legs.

"Good morning, Mum!"

"Good morning, koukla!" (Beautiful).

"Where's dad?"

"He…had to leave… early, didn't you hear him go out?"

"No, I didn't, Mum!" Hope replied looking unconvinced.

"Come on then love. Get up, go and get dressed and I'll prepare your breakfast"

"Can I stay in bed for five more minutes, please mum?"

"Okay, but I want you to be up in five minutes, 'because I don't want you to be late for school. What do you want for breakfast?"

"What can I have?"

"Whatever you want. Do you want some cereal or do you want an egg sandwich?"

"I'll have, uh, I'll have an egg sandwich please!"

After prying Hope off the toilet for the second time that morning, Hestia helped her put her black-hooded jacket on, tied her shoelaces and she said, "Come on, love." Hestia grabbed her car keys and they both made a mad dash for school. They still managed to get there on time, having only a few seconds to spare.

Hestia kissed Hope goodbye and decided to go into town as she couldn't face going back to that empty house with only her thoughts for company. At least in the town she could lose herself in the crowd.

As she parked the car in Linthorpe Road, she turned left towards the bank, then the demolition that was taking place behind Safeway supermarket distracted her. There was a row of old houses full of character where she and Zak had once discussed buying one when they would retire.

Those houses had now been knocked down and so had her dreams. The plans were to make the supermarket bigger, build a new petrol station and even more shops, as if there weren't enough already!

Her first stop was the bank to see if he'd left her any money for shopping and, as she handed her cash-card over, she knew that it was hopeless. But she had to try because they couldn't survive on fresh air.

The cashier, whose name tag said Shahin, looked from the computer screen to Hestia with a disdainful look and handed her card back.

Hestia shoved it in her purse, cursing Zak for putting her in that position again and walked out keeping her head low.

As she stepped into the street, she bumped into somebody and turned to apologise, then found herself staring up at a face that looked strikingly similar to Zak. She wondered if she had conjured him up with her thoughts.

As soon as she realised it wasn't him, she felt her cheeks grow hot with embarrassment and mumbled an apology. She walked away knowing he and his wives were staring at her retreating back.

The week had started badly and was steadily getting worse. Her concentration was now deteriorating and it was affecting her judgement. As she turned to cross the road, she glanced back to the bank and that man and his wives were still stood staring at her, not saying a word to each other, just staring.

Hestia felt an overwhelming need to escape their

dark stares. She took a deep breath and said to herself, help me God. She stepped out into the road, only thinking about putting distance between her and those strange people, not noticing the white Hyundai Lantra that she stepped out in front of, until the squeal of the brakes and the blaring of the horn brought her back to the present.

Embarrassed before, she was now mortified as the whole of the street stopped to look and see who was causing the commotion.

A voice from the crowd said, "Are you alright, love?"

Hestia smiled and mumbled "Yes, thanks."

Hestia ran across the road, all the while knowing hundreds of pairs of eyes were watching her every move, wondering what was wrong with her. She felt exposed and open and had a sudden need to be in familiar surroundings. She dashed to the library knowing that her haste drew more attention to herself. As she hurried into the library, she expected to find the peace and calm that she usually found there, but this time it was different. The silence that was usually soothing seemed almost loud and oppressive and the staff that went quietly about their work seemed to be in every aisle, studying her with surreptitious glances. She made an effort to relax and calm down as she felt things starting to get out of control.

Another member of staff appeared at the end of the bookcase.

Hestia picked up the first book she came to and stopped dead as she read the title: *"How to Be A Good Muslim."*

Out of all the books in the library, why did she pick up this one? Why did she stop at this shelf? At this bookcase? In this aisle? Was it subconscious or was there a deeper meaning? Was she led there? If so why?

She threw the book down and looked for another one, but they were all centered on Islam: *Why Islam?, The Islamic Religion, Never Without My Daughter, Muslims, Prophet Mohammed.*

She picked up each book and read the titles. There were so many, all saying the same thing. And they all had the same message for women: Conform, listen to what you are told, believe what you are told, do what you are told, wear what you are told, and never think for your self! No, no, no, this is not happening to me, no. Help me God. I'm going mad. It's not happening. All these books, all these titles, were all getting mixed up inside her head. What is happening to me? What is wrong? This must be a nightmare....i need to wake up! Things started to recede until all that was left in her line of vision was the book that seemed to be ruining her family's life:

The Koran!

Then, everything faded from view and she slipped into oblivion.

WEDNESDAY

---Invasion or A Plague---

Hestia's first conscious thoughts were, Where am I? Why can't I open my eyes? Why is there so much noise?

She was unsure if she had been asleep or not. Was she still asleep? Was she dreaming? No she couldn't have been. She was holding her breath and she was listening.

As she tried to raise her hand to her face, she realised there was something wrong with it. It felt heavy and uncoordinated. It landed heavily on her left cheek and she winced as she felt the bruise Zak had left on Monday and realised, she must have landed on it and compounded the injury.

She tried to raise her eyelids, but the light was blinding. A pain pierced through her skull, so she gave into the lethargy that seemed to have taken control of her body.

She lay there trying to distinguish between the various sounds that seemed to be coming from every direction. There were voices and beeps from machines and the clatter of things being moved, the swish of the curtains being yanked back and forth and suddenly it came to her. "Hospital," she mumbled very softly and very quietly. She was in hospital! Her eyes flew open and she made an effort to sit up, but her body refused to co-operate; as she lay there unable to move. Her white dressing gown lay across the end of her bed. The white pyjamas she now wore made her psychologically scared and emotional. Where exactly was she? What hospital was this? She assumed this was The General, but what if it wasn't? She could be in St. Luke's! (The mental clinic) She read an article about that place in the newspaper once. They had reported a man who thought he was receiving messages from God had finally snapped and tried to throw himself from the roof of the multi-story car park. They said he would be placed in St. Luke's secure section under suicide watch.

Had she finally snapped?

Zak had joked that time when she asked where St. Luke's was, that she would probably see more than enough of that place if she didn't relax and stop asking him questions or he would have her committed for paranoia.

It might have been a joke, but the thought of him being in control of her fate terrified her. Since that night, she had tried hard to restrain herself and her temper and only complain about things that he could not dispute. God help her and her children if that's what had happened to her. What would happen to the girls?

During one particularly nasty evening when Zak and Hestia had yet another argument, he had held her by the throat and told her the kids were his responsibility and he would do with them as he wished. If he wanted to, he could get out of the country within the hour and, by the time she had convinced the English Authorities to take any notice of her ranting, her precious kids would be safely in Libya with his family, and the girls married to good Muslim men.

God knows he had once tried it. It was the summer Athena had turned sixteen and Zak's sister, Fozia, and her extended family came to stay with them. Hestia and Zak had only just moved into their first house and nothing was really decorated, but when they came over, Hestia wouldn't dream of turning them away and made the best of a bad situation just like she always did.

Everyone had to double up beds and no one had any privacy. It was a squash, but Hestia had to grin and bear it or Zak would loose face, after all it was only for a week.

All went well, until the 6th day when everyone was invited to Hamida's for tea. It was while Hestia was helping Hamida prepare tea that she did the kindest thing she had ever done for Hestia.

Hamida stopped stirring the sauce and pushed it to the back of the hob, then took Hestia by the elbow and sat her down on one of the kitchen chairs. Shocked Hestia did as she was bid and Hamida glanced around to make sure they could not be overheard. Hestia started to get a bad feeling.

That feeling was swiftly conformed when Hamida said, "Look, Hestia, don't get annoyed, but I overheard Fozia talking to Zak and Mustafa and, from what I could understand, it sounded like they were arranging a match for Athena!"

"A match? What do you mean a match?"

"Well you know…a marriage!"

Hestia stared at Hamida and tried to decide

whether or not to believe her. After all they had only been true friends for the past year and to take her word over Zak's would mean she would have one of the biggest fights of her life on her hands. Only this time, it wouldn't just be with Zak, it would be against his whole family. It was the look on Hamida's face that finally convinced her and when she had made that decision, the reality of the situation actually sank in.

"What exactly did you hear?"

"Well, I didn't understand a lot of it but they mentioned Athena's name several times, that's what caught my attention and that's when I knew I should listen in. Fozia definitely said, 'That means, Athena and Adel should get married'"

"Yeah. Then what happened?"

"Then Zak said, that's a good idea, but when they noticed me by the door, Fozia said…and that means we'll do it Thursday?"

"Yes, so that's today!" said Hestia.

"I know. This is the first chance I've had to get you alone so I could tell you. So what can we do?" asked Hamida.

"My god. Do you think he'd do something like that to his daughter? Do you really think that he would do it without asking her? What kind of a father is he? Athena doesn't really know Adel. I'll tell you what, go tell Troy to start the car because Athena's not well. Then ask Athena to come here," said Hestia calmly.

"Okay," replied Hamida before rushing from the kitchen.

Athena came into the kitchen looking worried, followed by a flustered Hamida.

"What's wrong mum? Why is Troy in the car?" Athena enquired with a frown.

"You are going home. Pretend you are ill," stated Hestia firmly.

"What? Why? What's going on mum?"

"Don't ask, I'll tell you later. Just do as you're told and don't even say goodbye to anyone," said Hestia angrily.

"Okay, okay, mum" replied Athena quietly, as she walked through the door.

Hestia held the door ajar and watched as her daughter walked through the lounge, passed her father and aunt and out into the hallway. Hestia couldn't see any further than that, but she heard the car pull away and only then did she let the door close and sat heavily on her chair saying a silent prayer.

Zak accepted the simple explanation Hestia offered for Athena's absence, but when she kept to her room all through the final day of her aunt's stay, he made his displeasure known by picking fault with everything and everyone. It wasn't until evening when her aunt had left and Athena came downstairs that her father accused Athena of avoiding her aunt and her cousin, the same cousin they were trying to marry her off to.

Athena simply looked blank and replied that she couldn't help being ill. Zak obviously didn't believe her, but short of letting his intentions being known, there was very little he could do except storm about the house making the family miserable.

Hestia told Athena about his plans to marry her to Adel, and since that day Athena never looked at her father quite the same way.

Now with that memory in her head she felt the panic rise again and her breath came in short gasps and the incessant beeping increased in tempo.

The curtains were swiftly pulled back, to reveal a nurse of indistinguishable origin. Her swarthy complexions and dark eyes belied the fact that she came from Asia or Africa. Either way Hestia only saw the possibility of her being Muslim. In her confused mind, they seemed to be everywhere. It was like an invasion or a plague.

The nurse came forward and leaned over Hestia, mouthing words that her brain didn't register until she noticed the crucifix on her bosom.

Tears sprang in Hestia's eyes and rolled down her face.

The nurse murmured words of comfort as she wiped the tears away and habitually checked her vitals.

"Now, now, calm down, nothing bad is going to happen to you. I just need to ask you a few questions is that okay, Hestia? It is Hestia, isn't it?"

"Yes" Hestia replied. "What happened? Why am I here?"

"Well, you were brought in by the ambulance men because you lost consciousness in the library yesterday afternoon. Can you remember anything?"

"Where are the children?"

"The children have been informed. They came to see you yesterday and they are coming again later on. Now can you tell me what happened yesterday?"

"Yes…I…can…I…I…remember what happened…but I…I…" Hestia spoke in a soft voice.

"Let's start from the beginning, shall we?" the nurse replied.

"I…took my… younger daughter to school. I…kissed her good bye…and then I went…to town. I saw him, you know…it looked just like him…it wasn't him though. I could swear it was!"

"Now calm down, calm down. Look my name is Barbara and I'm one of the nurses who's been looking after you. We've had you sedated for most of the night, but you've tossed and turned, none-the-less and talked in your sleep. You obviously have a lot on your mind. Do you want to talk about it?"

"Yes," Hestia murmured.

"Who did you see, Hestia?" Barbara asked kindly.

"I saw…Zak. At least I thought I did," Hestia whispered.

"Who's Zak?"

"My husband."

"Oh, I see. Did you two argue?" suggested Barbara. "I know how that feels. Me and Jeff, my ex, we argued all the time. But it was always worst on the bairns. The things we put up with, believing 'it's all for the best', well don't let it get you down," said Barbara as she patted her hand.

"I try, but it's so hard. Then yesterday everything got so confusing and it felt like they were everywhere."

"Who?" asked Barbara slowly.

Hestia showed her face and realised how her answer would sound.

"Muslims," Hestia replied miserably.

"Oh…I see" said Barbara.

But Hestia could see that she plainly didn't.

"It's difficult to explain," said Hestia. She knew she was whining like Hope when she didn't get her own way. She sighed deeply and turned her head away.

Barbara sat on the edge of Hestia's bed and held

her hand. "Look Hestia, you've obviously been under a great deal of stress, and your body and mind having been trying to cope with it the only way they know how: by completely shutting down. It's not as uncommon as you think. All you needed is rest. Now, we've taken blood tests and they've all come back clear, but we'll do some more to rule out more complicated things. Now don't worry, we'll give you a prescription to take when you feel another panic attack coming on. These are quite strong tablets, but not so strong as to distort your perceptions or decisions. Now is there anything you don't understand?"

"No, only, did my husband come and see me?" asked Hestia warily.

"No, but I'm sure he'll be waiting for you at home." Barbara got up and smiled as she said this and, for the first time, Hestia realised she hoped never to see Zak again.

As Barbara pottered around the cubicle, Hestia was astounded by this thought. How could she think this? Easily, she answered herself. Look where you've ended up! Hospitalised! Oh no, not through the beatings he gave you, no, now he's messed with your mind. How you've managed this for so long is a miracle.

Hestia gave herself a mental shake. Stop talking to yourself. Or should she say stop answering herself?

God, she better fill that prescription and soon. Hestia closed her eyes and sighed.

Barbara noticed and smiled. "That's right, dear, you rest. The doctor will be round soon to see you and sign you out and your kids said they'll be here in an hour to pick you up."

Still smiling, Barbara left Hestia to her troubled thoughts.

The children arrived before the doctor. At the swish of the curtain, Hestia turned and saw Athena, Troy and Hope enter the cubicle. Athena came forward and gave a kiss and a hug to her mum. Hestia could see the worry in Athena's face, although she was smiling. Athena stepped back and Hope immediately rushed up to her mum. Hestia could not see her face for the bunch of flowers she was carrying. As Hope flung the flowers to the other side of the bed, she climbed up and threw herself at her mother and spontaneously burst into tears.

Hestia pried her off her neck and said, "Stop crying, 'because you'll make me cry as well!"

"I can't, Mum. I've missed you so much. I just can't stop crying! I want you to come home. I have really missed you."

"Of course you can, love. I'm coming home with you tonight so you can look after me!"

"Really mum?" asked Hope with a smile on her face.

"Yes, I never lie."

"Hi Mum," said Troy.

"Hi, love, how are you?"

"I'm fine. More to the point, how are you?"

"I'm feeling lots better, can't wait to go home!"

"So what happened? Have the doctors said anything? Can you go home tonight?"

"It was a panic attack, so they say…they have taken some blood for tests, they've given me an injection and some tablets to go home with."

"Hello there! How are you, Mrs Katti? Let me have a look at you. Oh yes, yes, yes, very nice. I think you are ready to go home, don't you? Yes? Good!" said a small Indian doctor, all in one breath, as he strutted into the cubicle. The family looked and smiled politely, waiting for someone to answer.

"And what's your name little girl?" he said to Hope who just stood and looked at him from behind Athena's legs.

"Oh well never mind, never mind. Now, Mrs Katti, you'll have to make sure you take things easy for a while. I'm sure your children and your little grand daughter will give you plenty of help, and you'll have to get plenty of rest. Is there anything you need to know before you go home?"

"No. Thank you very much, Doctor!"

"Good, good, good. If you need anything else, you know where to find us. Now take care of yourself and I hope I won't see you too soon. Good bye."

The doctor turned and strutted back out.

They all looked at each other and burst out laughing, which helped to ease the tension that had surrounded them since they'd entered the cubicle.

Then, Hope went over to her mum and said in an angry voice "but I'm not your granddaughter, Mum.

Why did he say that? You are my Mum!"

"Never mind. He didn't know love. He probably thought I was too old!" said Hestia and smiled.

"Yes but you're not. Mummy, are you?"

Barbara came in with Hestia's clothes as Troy made a hasty exit, dragging Hope with him to give Athena a chance to help her mum get dressed.

Barbara wheeled Hestia out in the wheelchair and into the waiting car where she hugged her and told her to take care of herself.

Hestia felt bereft with as she sat and watched Barbara through the back window. Although she'd only known her for a short period of time, she felt she was losing a kindred spirit and probably would never see her again.

The drive home was short, but it still exhausted her. Soon they reached home and she was safely installed in her bed.

"Mum? Do you want a hot chocolate?" asked Hope.

"No, love, I'm fine. I think I'll have an orange juice, so that I can have my tablets for the night."

"Okay then, I'll be up in two minutes with your orange juice."

"Mum, do you want the heating left on all night?" Athena asked quietly.

"I'm warm enough thanks, but you can turn the thermostat on 20 and then it'll stay warm all night. What do you think Athena?"

"If you wish, that's fine by me. Do you want me to bring you anything to eat or drink?"

"No thanks love, Hope is bringing me a glass of orange juice, so I can have my tablets."

"Okay then, I'm going to bed. Give me a shout if you need anything, I'll leave the doors open."

"Here you are, Mum. A glass of orange juice, a glass of milk just in case you feel thirsty in the middle of the night and here's a biscuit."

"Have you had your tablets, Hope?"

"Yes I just did. Mum? Can I sleep with you tonight?"

"Hope stop asking Mum. She needs some rest. She needs a break from all of us, especially you," Troy replied to his little sister.

"But Troy, just for tonight, please?"

"No! Come on, sis. Give Mum a hug and say good night. It's past your bedtime. Come on."

"Okay, then can I just read Mum a poem? Please, Mum, can I read you a poem?"

"Yes you can."

Hope gave her Mum a big kiss and said, "I'll just go and get it. Thank you, Mummy!" Hope couldn't hide her excitement.

"Right, are you ready Mum?"

"Yes, love, I'm listening."

Hope began.

"A heart that is as pure as gold,

"Brings joy and peace wherever she goes.

"Enjoys spending time with her family,

"Never overcome by daily stress.

"Very well organised and always in focus,

"She doesn't believe in violence or hatred.

"Her appearance is as a meadow of beauty,

"Quick on her feet solves every problem

"That the world will learn to live in peace."

Hestia had tears in her eyes as she softly

whispered, "That was a beautiful poem love. Well done."

"Come on, Sis, it's time for bed now. Say good night to Mum."

"Okay, good night, love you Mummy."

"Good night, love. I'll see you tomorrow morning bright and early."

"Goodnight."

One by one, the lights went out in the Kattis' household.

THURSDAY

---Stacks Of Paper---

Like a drowning sailor, Hestia fought her way to the surface of consciousness and desperately searched for a hold on reality. Her head ached with a slow dull thud, like the monotonous base of the funeral march. As she opened her eyes, pain lanced through her skull and left her feeling weak and nauseous.

I haven't felt this bad since I had morning sickness, she thought. Giving a small tight grin, she steeled herself, trying to rise.

The room tilted and swayed, but she gritted her teeth and waited for the world to settle, then tried to focus through slit eyes that felt very heavy and gritty. Her legs were only marginally better, in that they managed to get her from the bed to the bathroom and down the stairs.

Athena was already awake and preparing breakfast in the small, but airy kitchen and didn't notice her mother, until the feeling of being watched wormed its way through her busy brain.

She turned slightly, expecting to find an empty doorway, but jumped visibly and gasped when she encountered her mother's wan face several inches away. Athena automatically took a step backwards.

"Mum I nearly died!" Athena glared, then tempered her attitude when she noticed her mother's pallor and was instantly contrite.

"Come and sit down, Mum. I've made toast and tea," she said as she led Hestia to the table in the dining room.

"Oh, don't fuss love, I'm just a bit groggy after all that medication. All I need is a shower and then I'll have something to eat," she muttered.

"Well come on now, let's sort out the first thing that you need and get you some toast with chocolate spread and banana, 'because you need all the energy you can get," Athena said, as she sat her Mum to a seat, then turned to bring the toast and tea.

Athena poured the tea and added an extra spoonful of sugar for her mum as she looked like she needed it. While doing all this, she tried to observe her mother without being obvious and she didn't really like what she saw.

Her mother had always been considered a "Greek

beauty," and no one could hide their surprise when they found out she had two grown children. She looked a lot younger than her age and everyone complimented her on this, despite the fact that Hestia failed to accept that compliment and always put herself down by saying "they may say I look younger, but I don't really."

    She always looked after herself and wouldn't cross the doorstep without her hair or make-up done to perfection. Not that she was vain or anything like that, but more that she was proud and she would not dream of being anything less than she could possibly be. This would be like being unfaithful to herself and her family and nothing could be more important than family. Yes, Hestia strived to always do her best for them.

    But this morning, Athena clearly saw signs of stress on her mother's pinched face. The skin that was always smooth and soft was now dry and patchy and the olive tones were non existent. Now replaced by white and grey, they looked very pale.

    This was a situation she had never been placed in before. Hestia was always the strong one, the rock, for the whole family when pounded by their storm of a father. But now, Athena knew that role would have to be her.

Her mother looked like she would need some rest and quiet and, in order for this to happen, Athena would have to fill her mother's shoes without Hestia noticing.

A knock at the door, making them both jump. Athena looked anxiously from the door to her mum, and then rose to answer it.

As she peered around the front door the postman smiled and said, "Recorded delivery for Mrs. Katti!"

Athena relaxed a little bit and opened the front door wider, then took the clipboard the postman handed over and signed her mother's signature as she had done plenty of times before. As she handed the clipboard back, he handed her the letter over.

Athena quickly closed the door, then slowly walked back to the table where she placed the letter in front of her mother.

Hestia picked the brown envelope and studied it. She looked as if she was afraid of what it might contain. She turned it over in her hands, but there was no return address or any indication of where it might have come from.

She slipped her finger under the flap and ran it under the length of the flap until it was open. She slowly reached inside and pulled out a long white envelope. This was also plain until she turned it over and noticed a return address that read:

Rafferty & Co.

49 Baker Street

Durham City

County Durham

Her hands shook slightly, at the implications of this letter. She hesitantly opened the second envelope and drew out a thick, creamy sheaf of paper and read the first page in shocked silence.

"What is it, Mum?"

Silence followed.

"Mum, what does it say? What is it?"

Hestia just shook her head. She shook it again and continued to stare at the papers. It was a stack of papers!

Athena got up and walked around the table, to read over her mum's shoulder and was shocked to realize that it was DIVORCE papers. This was the last thing her mum needed right now, Athena thought to herself. How could this man be so insensitive, thoughtless, heartless and cruel to a woman who had given her whole life to him, to send her this without any prior knowledge, without even discussing it? After twenty odd years of marriage, they couldn't speak to each other. They couldn't even sit round the same table.

"Mum, listen to me. Mum, please look at me. He doesn't deserve you. If he wants a divorce, let him have it."

"Oh…I…wish I…could …"

"Mum just listen to me, that's the last thing you need right now. Ignore the letter for now, just for a few days 'until you are back on your feet and can think straight. Come on. You go and have a shower and I'll go and have a word with Troy."

"No…I'll sort it out. I can deal with it. You go and get ready for college…just leave."

"Mum, I'm only trying to help and I don't want you to be upset."

"I'm okay. Don't worry about me. I'll be all

right!"

Athena couldn't help but look at her mum and expected to see tears drop down her face, but it seemed as if all her tears had dried up. She seemed as if she didn't know what was happening.

"Mum, I won't go to college today. I'll give it a miss. I'll stay and keep you company."

"Don't be so daft…"

"I'm not being daft, Mum. I'm staying with you today and that's the end of it."

Athena reached across and took the papers out of her hand and put them back in the envelope, then helped her mum up from the table.

"Right. Go up and have a shower, Mum," she said and hustled her mum up the stairs.

As Hestia's shadow disappeared up the staircase, Athena picked up the envelope again and took a closer look at the letter as she scanned down the page. She passed the names and addresses until her eyes fell upon the word "*adultery*" and then stopped, unable to believe her own eyes.

How dare he? How dare he? How dare he even

suggest such a thing?

Her mother, who spent all her life looking after her family, who never stepped a foot out of the house unless she was with her children or him, where would she find the time? Why would she want to be with anyone else anyway, when she loved him so much? Her whole life was in that house with that family. She was the one who had to put up with his affairs, womanising, flirting, drinking, and drugs and pretend that he respected his religion? Hypocrite!

Her mum was always the one who was left behind waiting for him, not knowing where he was, what time he'd be back, who he was with or what he was doing.

Athena was disgusted. She never realised how low her father could go. It wasn't the first time he had accused her, but that was always in private when he knew he was losing an argument, whenever Hestia confronted him with his misdeeds, which he couldn't explain away. He always twisted the facts around and began slinging accusations at Hestia.

He always started with simple ones: you don't

love me, you don't want to be with me, you want to be with someone who is English. In fact, I've been told you have an English boyfriend, and then his temper would rise and the accusations would get wilder and wilder.

He sounded like a raving lunatic, making up his own conspiracy theories, bordering on hysteria, so that Hestia ended up having to defend herself against her husbands' paranoia.

Athena was furious. He was always like a child, demanding what he wanted instead of asking, he was taking and not offering anything in return, committing every type of social faux pas and not considering anyone else's feelings or comforts. His own insecurities made his behaviour even more and more unstable. Because of this, the lives of his family became harder to bear. He kept every single family member on a tight reign and none were allowed any sort of freedom, especially his wife. That's how he thought of her. Not as Hestia. Not as a woman. Not as the mother of his children, but his wife, his property just like every other Muslim man would....wife would equal to property!

This train of thought was making Athena's blood

boil. She knew she should try and calm down, but it had gone too far. It was as if she had no power to control this terrible urge to hurt or destroy something or someone.

She turned away from the table in hopes of banishing that vile word from her mind. That one simple word that had ignited this anger that now consumed her, she cast about for an avenue to vent this fury. Her gaze fell upon her father's watch which was on the mantle piece .

She snatched it up and smiled with malice at the thought of destroying his favourite trinket he bought with the money he should've spent on his wife's anniversary present. This small object represented all her father's real priorities and became the symbol of his vanity, his pride and the deceit he represented to the rest of the world whilst creating his own private purgatory with which he controlled his family.

She marched into the kitchen and grabbed the hammer from the cupboard under the sink. She then looked at the watch and then stormed through the back door whilst the fury still had hold of her feelings.

Athena dropped to her knees, unaware of the damp that penetrated her black jeans from the rain soaked concrete.

The watch disintegrated with the first blow, but that didn't satisfy the need to destroy this object that symbolised so much misery her family, and especially her mum, had gone through in order for Zak to appear prosperous and well to do. The meagre meals, the lack of money for petrol, food or anything he considered unnecessary.

Athena didn't notice the tears streaming down her face, nor the voice that was calling her name over and over again.

Hope was stood in the doorway unable and unwilling to come any closer to the vicious swings of the black and silver hammer. She stood screaming Athena's name, and it was a full 30 seconds until her high-pitched wails pierced the red haze that filled Athena's mind.

The hammer paused in mid flight, and then as swiftly as it all began, it ceased and all that she was left with was a hollow feeling and one mangled watch.

Athena crawled towards Hope to comfort her and reassure her, but Troy beat her to it.

"What's wrong, Hope? What's going on? Are you okay? Athena?"

"Troy!"

"What's going on, Athena?"

"I don't know," Athena said in tears.

"Come on, Hope, shhh now, now stop crying, I'm here. Shhh, no need to cry. I'm here. What happened, Athena?"

"I don't know what's come over me Troy. I honestly don't know."

"Where's Mum?"

"She's upstairs. She's having a bath and…"

"Will you tell me what happened. Athena?" asked Troy angrily.

Hope then replied "I came downstairs…and I saw… Athena smashing… something outside…she was…she was…"

Troy took a step closer to the door that lead to the garden, where Athena was still kneeling.

He had a look and softly he asked Athena once again, "What's going on, Sis? What happened?"

"Mum will tell you later, I don't think it's up to

me to tell you, Troy. I think you should wait until Mum gets out of the bathroom and then she'll tell you."

"What are you talking about, Sis?"

Athena looked at Troy and Hope as she heard her mother's footsteps coming closer.

"What's happened?" Hestia asked, looking shocked.

They all looked at each other as Troy handed Hope back to Hestia and then helped his sister get back to her feet and sat her on the wooden chair in the dinning table.

Troy asked, "Will someone please tell me what is going on?"

Hestia took a deep breath; leaned forward, picked up the envelope and handed it over to Troy.

Troy pulled out the forms and read without speaking, while the rest sat quietly waiting for the final explosion.

All eyes were on Troy as they all expected him to blow his top off, even though he was very laid back except for one thing that really angered him: any attack on his family, especially his mother, in any shape or form.

He eventually sat down and started to re-read the forms, this time more intensely. His face was a study in concentration, and growing visibly more and more grim.

Troy looked up and stared intently at his mother, then said quietly, "I can't believe my eyes, I'm so sick…so angry…I…I…I'm so annoyed with what I'm reading. It's…it's…not true! He's lying, Mum…he's just lying about everything…he's…he's…oh god what can I say? I just can't believe he'd lie like this."

Troy put the papers down, then took hold of his sister. Athena allowed Troy to lead her up the stairs hence giving Hestia the peace and quiet she needed to face the divorce papers lying in front of her.

Athena sat on her bed listening to Troy's soothing words, which could be heard through the thin walls of the adjoining bedrooms. She felt acute shame at having lost control of herself. How many times had she sneered at her father's lack of control over his temper, over the fact he flew into blind rages in the blink of an eye, but hadn't she just done the same thing herself? Hadn't she shown just how alike she was to the father she despised?

Beyond all else this thought sickened her. How hard she tried to be calm and rational like her mother, to be the mediator in the family, to find solutions to the problems they faced. Her mother always seemed to do these things without effort and Athena tried her hardest to emulate her mother's natural talent, but all too often, her more instinctive temper got the better of her. Her only compensation was knowing that, unlike her father, she possessed a conscience and would bitterly regret her hasty words and actions, and that she could apologise as swiftly as she could calm down.

    She dragged herself from her bed and made an attempt to shake off this dark mood that seemed to have settled upon her. Hurriedly, she dressed in her usual black attire, realising that Hope had very little time in which to make it to school, without having yet another black mark against her name for being late.

    Athena emerged from the bathroom refreshed and outwardly calm and in better control of her emotions than she had been for the past 48 hours.

    Hope left the bathroom, at the same time, and there was an uneasy moment when she looked at Athena without trust. This didn't go unnoticed by her older sister, so she cast about desperately for a way to lighten the mood.

"Come on squirt, time for school! Go grab your bag and give Mum a kiss or we'll be late!"

Hope grinned with relief. This was the sister she knew and loved, not that wild creature on her knees in the yard. She ran down the stairs as fast as her thin awkward legs could carry her, knowing her sister would be right behind her trying to catch her and kick her up the bum. Not that she ever did, but it was a reassuring ritual and she loved her sister for playing with her.

Hestia was still seated at the table. Her mind was, God only knew where, so she jumped when Hope threw herself at her for a farewell kiss.

"Oh are you going, Love?" asked Hestia in a monotone voice.

"Yep, Athena's driving me today. Can she pick me up too please?" Hope pleaded.

"Well, I don't see why not, but it'll all depend on who's busy and who's not. Now, have you got all your things?" Hestia asked.

"Yes," sighed Hope.

"Okay then off you pop and don't worry about your sister. You know she's a loony" Hestia joked loud enough for Athena to hear.

"Yeah, I know, it runs in the family," replied Athena from the front doorway as she stepped outside.

"Bye Mum," giggled Hope.

"Bye love," said Hestia.

"I won't be too long, Mum. Do we need anything from the shop?" asked Athena

"No, we'll go to the shops later," Hestia said.

"Okay, bye," said Athena.

With that, Athena left the house, then helped Hope into the car, making sure to fasten her seatbelt.

The short journey was filled with Hope's incessant chatter on the all-important Sabrina the Teenage Witch.

This lasted right up to the school gate where the teacher stood, blowing on the whistle to call in the students.

Hope skipped happily inside with her pal and Athena found herself, for the first time in her life, wishing she were yet again a child without the responsibilities of knowing the truth of her parent's relationship.

    Athena lost sight of Hope as she disappeared into the school.

FRIDAY

---The Facts---

Athena drove home, knowing she had to motivate her mother into action, never having she seen her mum so stunned, so at a total loss, so unsure of her future. Athena knew what decision should be made, but could she persuade her mother to stand up to her violent husband? Even though he was the one to initiate divorce proceedings, Athena knew it was an empty threat, but he knew Hestia would not realise this. Therefore, she would be devastated and unstable. He knew the right buttons to push!

The only thing Hestia took a stand on, against her husband, was her children. She took the punishments for imaginary wrongs, humiliations in front of his Muslim friends for overstepping his religious boundaries. She did all this in order to keep her family together.

Athena knew now was the time to fight for whatever was left of her family and her life. She knew how innately weak her mother was when it came to Zak, but she also knew that, if supported, her mother could become again that fearless creature that dazzled all who beheld her. After all, wasn't that exactly what had happened to her father when he met Athena's mother? Wasn't he so overcome with her presence that he vowed to possess her and make her his, even if it meant lying and cheating to accomplish the deed? He lied about his faith, he lied about his family, he told Hestia he was a Christian Catholic! He presented Hestia with people he hardly knew as his family only for the wedding to go ahead!

Well Athena thought to herself, if it took bullying and badgering to make her mother act, then she would do just that, but this time it would not be tainted with hate and cruelty, it would be tempered with love and support.

So with an air of determination, Athena slammed the car door and strolled up the path to rally her mother.

"Well what are you going to do about it all, Mum?"

"I don't know yet."

"Yes you bloody do know. I'm sick of him trying to ruin our lives. We have no friends because he doesn't allow us to have any friends, we have different identities because he doesn't want us to be Greek and Christian Orthodox, we cannot speak to people just in case he sees us and becomes paranoid that I have a boyfriend or you have an affair, we are not allowed out of the house unless we have the "OK" from him to do it, he locks us in the house just because he feels like it, we have no money, because he wants to control us! I'm sick of you making excuses for him, trying to be nice about everything and forgive him every time he says sorry. This is not right, Mum. Not right for you, not right for us, especially Hope!"

"Don't say things like that Athena. I'm trying to do what's best for everyone."

"No you're not, Mum. You are trying to do what's best for him!"

"Athena stop it!" Hestia replied, with tears in her eyes.

"No I won't stop, Mum. It's about time you took back control of your life. You've spent so long letting him make all the decisions that you've forgotten how to do it for yourself and now, when you've got the most important decision in your life to make, you can't do it. What are you going to do? Are you going to ask him to make the decision for you? He's already made up his mind; you've got the proof of that right in front of you. Now it's your chance, Mum. It's your chance to do something for you and your children instead of for him. You can be free. Its like living in prison without fences."

Hestia looked Athena in the eye and said in a vicious whisper, "Everything I've done, I've done it for my children, not for him, not for me, but for you!"

"No you didn't. You always say that. That's always your answer when we argue about him. He's lied, he's cheated, he's been unfaithful, he's hit you, he's hit your children and not because he was angry, but he had thought about it and then beat everyone because he enjoyed it! And you're still willing to ignore it and pretend it hasn't happened. You are prepared to live the rest of your life with him? Well I'm sorry but I 'm not! Either he goes or we go! Because I'm telling you now, Mum, Troy won't stay either and then it will only be you and Hope left, or maybe that's what you want!"

"Stop it! Now you've gone too far!"

"No, Mum, it's you who's not gone far enough! What's it going to take to make you realise, he's not the man you married? He's not that soft-spoken Adonis you fell in love with. That man was never real. He lied to get a ring on your finger and once he did, the fairytale ended. Take a good look at him and see what you've ended up with!"

"Don't be ridiculous, he's not that bad."

"Right! Tell me one good thing about him then, huh Mum?"

"Well, he's…he's your dad. I don't have to list his qualities."

"I'm sorry to tell you, Mum, but he stopped being my father the day he took the tennis racquet to my face and told me it was for my own good. The day he punched me on my face and let me bleed for hours on end. The day he had his hand round my throat squeezing so tight I couldn't breath. All in the name of the Koran. That's not the actions of a good father, not a sane one anyway."

"Exactly. He's not himself. He needs help and support from his family. He's had a lot of problems."

"We've all had the same problems, Mum, in case you haven't noticed. We've been through everything he's been through, but we are not drug addicts just like him. We don't sleep around with anyone who would let us just like he does. We don't steal from the family just like he does, we don't lie and, most of all, we don't beat each other up just because we had a bad day at college or a bad day at work!"

"Now you're exaggerating."

"Am I? Tell me one thing that I mentioned that's not true. Come on, Mum, tell me. No you can't, so don't even try."

"Okay, okay, I know you're right, but what can I do about it? I cant leave him. We have nothing without your dad. He is the one that looks after us all, he provides for us. I cant survive without him".

"What are you talking about mum? Of course you can. You need to break free from these chains that have trapped you in his hands for years. Who said you cant do anything without him? You can start by signing the fucking divorce papers!"

Hestia looked at her daughter in disbelief that she

had just swore. "Athena, there is no need to swear."

"Never mind my language, what about those papers?"

"I don't know Athena, I've got to think about this!"

"What's there to think about? You finally admitted to yourself what a twat he is, but you still dithering. Don't you see he knows you're not going to sign the papers? That's why he sent them. He still thinks you can't live without him. All the crap he s been putting in your head, I know what he s been saying to you mum. I know he s told you that you are nothing without him. But here's your chance to prove him wrong! I am working every evening, I am at college in the morning, we can manage perfectly without him, trust me mum, have I ever let you down?"

Hestia stopped and stared at her daughter as if seeing her for the first time. Where had her little girl gone? Is this young woman that's giving her advice really her daughter? Surely it should've been the other way around. Why had she not noticed how grown up she was? Hestia knew that Athena had the best interests at heart. But would she be strong enough to make it on her own without him?

Athena watched the expressions play across her mother's face and understood the emotions that lay beneath.

She stepped up to her mum and gave her a hug, then whispered in her ear, "You'll never be alone, Mum. You'll always have me, no matter what happens. I love you and I know it's hard, but you have to do the right thing. We'll never leave you! I will ALWAYS look after you!"

As Hestia opened her mouth to reply, the phone rang. She leaned backwards to answer it.

"Hi Hamida!" she said looking significantly at Athena.

Athena smiled and mouthed, "I'll go make some lunch." She walked to the kitchen, smiling to herself.

Although Hamida was loved by all the family, Athena knew this phone call could last for hours, so she set about making sandwiches for lunch.

Hamida, who's real name was Linda, was a lovely person who was the life and soul of the party.

Guaranteed to have all the gossip, she was just as good at collecting it as she was at dishing it out. But apart from all this, she was the only friend Hestia was allowed to have.

Although Hamida was an English girl she had converted to Islam at the age of seventeen when she married Zak's younger brother, Mustafa. Her life was a little better than Hestia's, but she was more resigned to it after having four boys in ten years, much to Mustafa's delight.

Boys were highly prized amongst the Muslim community, where girls were thought of as a little more than a way of joining families together and were barely tolerated.

Hamida, nevertheless, loved every single one of her boys and spent all of her time with them. Despite her gossiping nature, she and Hestia had developed a genuine bond that went beyond friendship. Their age gap made no difference to the two friends, who found comfort in each others misfortunes that echoed similarly in both their lives. Whatever one endured, the other was bound to have had some sort of experience in.

As Athena made the essential cup of tea to go with their lunch, she caught enough snatches of the conversation going on in the other room to know that Hestia was spilling her guts to Hamida, who would be telling her to make up her own mind and not to be swayed by her children or her husband.

Athena dreaded thinking about what might be going through Hestia's mind. Not being privy to the conversation that was going on between the friends, she had no idea what Hestia's final decision would be.

As Athena carried the sandwiches to the table, Hestia stopped talking, making it obvious to Athena that whatever was being said was not meant for her ears. Her mother hastily made her farewells and replaced the handset.

Athena, determined to have at least one quiet hour for lunch, decided not to mention the obvious snub, so she put MTV on.

"What's in the sandwich love?"

"Just cheese and tomato, Mum. I didn't know if you wanted anything else. Is that okay for you?"

"Yes, that's lovely!"

"Do you remember when we were in Greece, Mum, when you told me to take the video back to the video shop and I wanted to go on Troy's bike?"

"Yes, I remember when you fell off the bike and…."

"And I was taken to hospital. Aunt Dora came to pick you up, didn't she?"

"Yes, I was waiting at the balcony for you because I knew…I knew…there was something wrong…and when I saw you in Dora's car I just knew that something had happened to you."

"How many stitches did I have?"

"About eight I think."

"What a day!"

"Do you remember the afternoon that you went to take some food to the dog?" said Hestia to Athena.

"I do, yes, when I got bit…I remember I asked you not to tell dad and, as soon as I showed you my wound, you went ballistic."

"It was bad though. We had to take you to the hospital and I couldn't have taken you by myself."

"What a year that was, I was accident-prone."

"Years go by so quickly and life passes us by. We ask why things happen to us, but I suppose everything happens for a reason."

"We are put on this earth for a reason and…"

"Yes everyone has a reason for living. Sometimes I think to myself what is ours? Think of the world, Athena, going round and round in space. No one knows how it all started or how we began, yet people all over the world fight about religion and never stop to think how lucky we are to be healthy and alive."

Hestia was right; every word she spoke was true. Still her world stood still every time she thought of Zak, every time she looked at the papers that were on top of the coffee table.

"Right, Mum, nothing needs to be decided today. Let's just relax and forget about it all. We'll try and have a normal day and give the house a spring cleaning." Athena said, trying to sound positive.

"Okay, love. We'll make a start downstairs first and then we'll work our way up," replied Hestia through a mouthful of sandwich.

Athena smiled, thinking her mum looked better

than she had all morning. So as Hestia took the dirty pots to the sink. Athena plugged in the hoover and picked everything off the floor. As Athena vacuumed the carpet, Hestia removed the cushions from the sofa, so Athena could vacuum there as well.

Hestia went and picked up the cushions from her favourite chair, only to stop with the last cushion still in her hand. "Come on daydream, move over," said Athena, but Hestia just looked at Athena. With a sigh, Hestia bent down and picked something up from the bottom of the chair. She handed it to Athena and sat down heavily on the now empty seat.

Athena turned over the Dictaphone and looked questioningly at her Mum, who just shrugged her shoulders and said "Guess who put that there?"

"You must be joking! What does he expect to hear?" Athena asked amazed.

"Who knows? Let's listen to it and find out," said Hestia, remarkably calm.

Athena didn't know if this was a good sign or not, but did as she was asked.

As the tape rewound they waited impatiently

until it stopped. Athena pressed the PLAY button with her index finger that shook ever so slightly. The whir of the tape was the only sound in the silent room and they both held their breath and waited.

"I've been out all day…"

"That's dad!"

"Shhh, listen."

"And you've prepared fish and chips…"

"When was that, Mum?"

"Shh."

"Zak, stop it!"

"That's you," said Athena.

"Shh, turn it off. I don't want to hear it," said Hestia reaching for the tape.

"Well I do," said Athena moving it out of her mother's reach.

S L A P!!

"What was that?" exclaimed Athena. "Did he hit you again? Eh? When was this, Monday?" Athena asked.

"Oh just forget it."

"No I won't. When was it? Monday?"

"Yes, now stop shouting at me!"

"Okay, I'm sorry. But he came home and the first thing he did was plant a tape recorder in a chair that only you ever sit on. Who does he think he is, James fucking Bond? Then he picks an argument and then he slaps you again and you say forget about it? What's it going to take for you to see that he is not normal mum! He's sick. How can you say that you still love him?"

Athena glared at her mother, breathing heavily after her outburst. She knew she was being unfair to her mother who was still in a fragile state, but things were going from bad to worse and something had to be done.

She knew she couldn't force her mum, but she could point out the facts that her mum kept glossing over.

Hestia stared at the tape as if she couldn't quite believe what she was hearing. It was obvious that her emotions were in turmoil.

Athena kept quiet, hoping her mum would see things the way they really were and not the way she wanted them to be.

She reached for the tape recorder with the

intention of distraction, only to be thwarted in her attempt by Athena's quick reflexes and her even quicker mind that seemed to process things even when occupied with several other tasks.

"No, Mum, don't. This is evidence"

"Give it to me then, Athena."

"No think about it. We can use this. If he can tape you, you can tape him!"

"What are you talking about? I don't even know where he is, let alone if he's coming back."

"He always does! Who's to say that this is the only one? Save your energy. We have a lot to do before Hope comes home! We've got about an hour, so let's finish off here and start in the kitchen."

"You think that there could be more, Athena?"

"Why not? We don't know until we look. Come on, Mum," said Athena, hauling the cushions back onto the chair. "This is going to take a while."

Hestia and Athena spent the next hour and a half, first turning the lounge and then the kitchen upside down. Putting everything back together again, they only had one Dictaphone to show for all their efforts.

Hestia was the first one to stop tidying and realised that they were already five minutes late to pick up Hope. "Athena look at the time! Leave all that. I'll do it. You go and get your sister, but drive carefully!"

"Oh God, we forgot the time! Right. I'm gone. See you soon. Glad it was only one, Mum!" Athena said as she pecked her mum goodbye.

Hestia made a face at her daughter as she left; she was determined to brave it all out.

As Athena disappeared out the door, Hestia let out a sigh of exhaustion she didn't realise she had been holding in for the last two hours. She sank into her favourite chair and relaxed for what seemed like the first time since she had risen that morning. She couldn't totally release all the tension in her body, but the few minutes she had to herself felt like bliss and she savoured every moment.

With her head laid back and her eyes wide shut she made a conscious effort to clear her mind of all thoughts and concentrated on her favourite memory that had always managed to calm her and lift her spirits.

She was 13-years-old and overflowing with

hormones and emotions. Her mother and father sat at a table, sharing an ice-cream sundae. With only one spoon, they fed each other.

    Hestia sat atop a wall that surrounded the small, but exclusive, café at the summit of the mount, in the middle of the ancient part of Athens. She stared across the city, to the only other mount of the same considerable size. The Acropolis.

    The sun shown its last rays of the day while the white marble of the columns shone with an unnatural iridescence that hurt their eyes. Giving that sacred place an eerie glow, Hestia shivered in the light as she imagined the priestesses and handmaidens that once prayed to those fickle gods and goddesses, making sacrifices in order to secure a fruitful harvest or marriage.

    As the lights slowly faded to gold, the atmosphere of the whole city changed. Gone was the slow-packed life that plodded on at a snail's pace, a pace that suited everybody in that hot climate, only to be replaced by lights, food, wine, music, laughter and noise. It was as if the Greeks had swapped one form of heat for another and intended to use this cool heat to their full advantage. People worked hard all day and partied harder for most of the nights. This had been the same since the birth of this great civilisation and Hestia loved to watch the transformation from her high perch, so close to the gods and goddesses that she felt such an infinity with them.

She felt like a queen, seated higher than everyone else, answerable only to herself and the dieters. In full control of her life she loved, living in a place she loved, with people she loved. Nowhere and at no time would she be happier than here and now. This was her perfect time, her perfect place. This was Heaven!

As Athena entered the lounge she smiled at the sight that met her. Her mother was sound asleep on her chair, looking relaxed and peaceful. Athena turned and raised her finger to her lips at Hope, who looked passed her sister and giggled at the unfamiliar sight of her mother sleeping during the day.

Athena motioned for Hope to backtrack and they made their way back outside, closing the front door very softly; only to jump a mile as Troy jumped out from around the corner.

"Boo! Ha ha ! What are you up to?" Troy said gleefully.

"Shh, you stupid sod. We nearly died! Mum's asleep, so we are going for a McDonald's," replied Athena with a frown.

"Are we?" said Hope excitedly.

"Mum's asleep? Why is she asleep? Is she ill?" asked Troy.

"No she's stressed and hasn't been sleeping well lately, not that you would have noticed!"

"Well, why should I have?" grumbled Troy.

"Well, I did, so you should have," said Athena.

"Are we going now or what?" asked Hope, again trying to turn the conversation to the way she wanted it to go.

Athena and Troy shared an amused look as each grabbed one of Hopes hands and swung her high in the air while she squealed with joy.

"Yes, young lady we are going!"

"We'll take my car, Athena. It's better than yours," Troy said, giving Athena a sideways glance. He always knew this sparked a competitive streak.

Athena took a swipe at him, over Hope's head that he easily ducked.

The three of them didn't arrive back home until six-o clock, carrying a bag of junk food for their mum and chocolate and caramel sundaes for afters. The house was still in darkness as they entered so they tread softly so as not to startle Hestia when she'd wake up.

Athena switched on the lights and Hestia blinked, then looked around not realising she had fallen asleep. "What time is it love?" she asked sleepily.

"It's five past six," Troy replied "You should be ashamed of yourself, neglecting your children. We had to feed ourselves and all sorts of stuff!"

"Yeah? Well, how was Mr McDonald's?" she replied, knowing full well where they had been.

"He's fine, he sent you some tea over and I'll set it on the table for you and Athena will make the coffee…"

"Cheeky git…"

"Ooh, ooh, Athena," gasped Hope.

"You sit down and eat your ice cream smelly,"

teased Athena.

"Mum, tell her…"

"Athena, stop winding her up!" Hestia said.

"I always get the blame," said a voice from the kitchen.

"Just make the coffee fatty," said Troy.

"Troy…stop it…,"said Hestia as Hope giggled.

"What, ugly?" said Troy to his mother, as Hestia threw a cushion at him and missed, but hit Hope squarely in the face.

"Ow! Mum! What did I do?" complained Hope throwing it back.

"That was pathetic smelly," said Athena as she placed the mugs on the table.

"Oh God, couldn't you have all stayed at McDonald's?"

"What and let you sleep all day? We know you need your beauty sleep, but this is ridiculous! Stop complaining and eat your burger…ugly!"

Hestia knew she was outnumbered, so she accepted the goody bag Hope had thrust at her, then smiled at the warm fries and slightly squashed burger.

"Thanks, smelly!"

"Mum!"

They all sat round the table and enjoyed the easy going mood while it lasted.

"Have you got any homework love?"

"Yeah."

"Off you go, upstairs then, and shout to me if you need any help."

"Can I do it later, Mum?"

"No, you'll have to do it now sweetie!"

"Okay, but can I do my homework down here then?"

"No, love. You know the rules, upstairs where you can concentrate."

"Okay," she grumbled.

Athena waited a while until she heard Hope's door shut and then she said, "Are you going to tell Troy, Mum?"

"Tell me what?"

"Where did you put it, Athena?"

"It's here in my bag, Mum!" said Athena as she took it and placed it on the table.

"Whose is that?"

"It's not mums and it's not mine. And, it's obviously not yours so…"

"Where was it?"

"It was beneath the cushion's in mum's chair"

"What's on it?"

"Just an argument we had when he came in on Monday. He must have put it there as soon as he was alone," said Hestia hurriedly.

"What are you going to do about it? Will you have a word with dad?"

"I don't know," said Hestia.

"Well I do!" replied Athena "We are going to use it on him. He only comes back to use the phone and, when he does, he only speaks in Arabic with the door shut, so no one can listen. I think that some thing's going on. He's been acting strange all week and now this!"

"We can't do that. What if he finds it?"

"He won't! We'll hide it where he won't find it."

"Where?"

"Let's go and have a look," said Athena, standing, then walking to the garage that had been converted to an extra study.

The others followed her, but stayed on the threshold, unwilling to enter his domain. The room was always considered Zak's private territory and the only one allowed to enter was Hope, who was his favourite.

As she looked around the room for a hiding place for the Dictaphone, she discounted everything on the desk as being too obvious and noticeable.

Where would he not look, she thought to herself. Underneath the carpet? Behind his desk? Where could they put the Dictaphone? Where would he not look? Where would be close enough to hear his conversations without him knowing where it was?

Athena stood in the centre of the room, underneath the light. Slowly turning, she chose and then dismissed each hiding place. His desk was out of the question as were his bookshelves and filing cabinets. The only other objects were the sofa bed and the toy box that was neatly behind the door.

On the sofa bed sat Hope's favourite dolls and an old teddy her father had won for her at the fair about three years earlier. It had been loved to death and was waiting treatment in Hope's "hospital" that was now the sofa bed. Its left leg was split and its right ear was torn and hanging off. Athena picked up the bear and stuck a finger in the split leg, then poked around.

"You are not serious," said Troy.

"Why not?" she replied. "Hand it over and I'll see if it'll fit." said Hestia.

"It'll muffle the voices. You won't be able to hear a word. This is stupid, Sis. Come on now," Troy retorted.

"We'll try it and see. Look, it fits perfect. Hang on while I get it in the right place. There! All set. See? You go and sit in dad's chair and talk to us."

Troy looked doubtful, but he wanted to prove his point, so he sat gingerly in his father's chair as if it would suddenly grab him.

"Well, go on then, talk to me!" Athena snapped at her reluctant brother.

"Don't you have to press record?"

"Its voice activated, dummy! Just start talking and it starts itself!"

"What do you want me to say?" He moaned.

"Anything. Tell us about college or your lovely car."

"Okay. My car, for a start, it's better than yours."

"Oh! Ha ha! Change the record," Athena said

"Oh, for goodness sake, take the thing out and rewind it so we can listen," begged Hestia, as things started getting out of control.

Athena retrieved the tape and rewound it back, then pressed "play" while the other two listened, one hopeful while the other one was doubtful.

"Well go on then talk to me," Athena's voice came out loud and clear. "What do you want me to say," replied Troy's voice, slightly quieter.

"See?" said Athena, looking very smug. "I told you, it is the perfect place! He ll never even notice the difference."

"That's great. We'll put it there. Give it to me and I'll stitch it up, just in case." Said Hestia.

"In case of what? Mum?"

"Just in case, pass it here."

Hestia took the injured teddy and proceeded to

set it, and position the Dictaphone, inside the leg of the teddy bear. When it was to her liking, she took needle and thread and started to stitch up the poor teddy.

Hestia looked up at her two children, who watched her as if they had never seen her sew before. She smiled to herself. They all saw this as a game which, if she was honest, she would rather it be for them. She wanted to spare them the heartache and the stress she felt every time something happened between her and Zak.

When she was finished, she took the bear and placed him back between the other patients at Hope's "hospital", then glanced around to ensure that nothing was out of place. When she was satisfied with her inspection, she closed the door, knowing that it would be days before Zak decided to return and even if he did, would he use the phone? She prayed the batteries didn't run out and hoped Zak would return and use the phone very soon.

Her prayers were answered sooner than she was ready for. At half past seven, just as they all sat down to watch EastEnders, four heads turned in union towards the front door in response to the distinct sound of keys in the lock.

"Act normal," hissed Hestia as she turned up the TV volume.

Zak entered the lounge and looked around at his family who completely ignored him with the exception of Hope who smiled at him.

He sent her a smile back as he ruffled her thick curtain of hair and passed her by to enter his study, then closed the door without uttering so much as a word of greeting.

As the door clicked shut Athena and Troy turned to look at their mother who nodded towards the TV as if to say wait. The tension was terrible and still Hestia sat seemingly motionless in her chair staring at the screen.

Hope fidgeted, Athena huffed and sighed, Troy kept his eyes fixed on the study door, but neither of them spoke one word, not one word. This was the effect one man, their father, could have on his own children, who had earlier been joking, giggling and carefree. Now they were tense, strained and silent, desperate for the situation to be over.

As the credits rolled down the screen and the familiar music died to a momentary silence, Zak's voice was heard by all, the meaning of the words lost in an ancient language that no one in the lounge had mastered, but all the same they all heard his voice, deep rich, and knew he was bringing his conversation to an end.

"Do you want a coffee, Mum?" Athena asked as she made the rise.

"No. Stay where you are. If you make coffee, he might decide to stay and talk. I want him to go, so we can see what he had to say," said Hestia quietly.

"How are you going to see what he said if you are not going to talk to him, Mummy?" asked Hope innocently.

Hestia stared at Hope realising she had spoken without thinking, and doing that in front of such an inquisitive child could be disastrous to everyone. "Never you mind, just be quiet," she snapped.

At that point, Zak emerged from the study avoiding eye contact with anyone and disappeared up the stairs.

Still no one spoke, but continued to watch TV,

without taking any notice of the police drama. It was over an hour later that Zak descended the stairs after taking a shower and changing his clothes. His other ones most likely left on the bathroom floor to be washed by his obedient wife.

Hestia did let his arrogance goad her into wanting to voice her irritation, but she held her tongue until he collected his coat and departed as silently as he had arrived.

All eyes darted to Hestia, who sat as comfortably still as if she hadn't even noticed Zak's departure. Then, slowly, she eased herself from her seat as though she had sat too long and made her way to the front window and surreptitiously peered through the blinds as she pulled the cord to close them. Hestia then walked to the front door and threw the bolt across and locked the dead bolt. Then, and only then, when she felt secure in her own mind that he could not come back in and find out their plot, did she open the study door. She switched on the light, but stopped before she crossed the threshold. Turning around, she said, "Athena, take Hope up to bed, please, and then we have work to do."

"Oh, Mum, do I have to?" moaned Hope.

"Yes you do. Now, give everyone a kiss goodnight," said Hestia

"Okay. Goodnight, Mum. Goodnight, Troy," said Hope trying to stifle a yawn.

"Come on, Sis, you re nearly asleep already," urged Athena as she carried Hope out of the room, only to return in a record of approximately one minute.

"Have you got it?"

"Yeah, come and sit down and see if we can understand what's been said."

Athena sat on one side of her mother while Tory sat on the other as Hestia removed the tape. All three concentrated and tried to understand Zak's voice as the tape begun to play.

"Mum, can you understand anything?"

"I haven't got a clue. There's a few words, but none make any sense."

"Who can we trust that knows Arabic and can translate?" Troy asked.

There's always Hamida," Athena replied.

"It's far too late to be bothering Hamida this time

of the night," said Hestia.

"Well, we can't do anything tonight then, Mum, 'because we can't understand. We should have another go tomorrow morning."

"We'll go to Hamida's in the morning because I know Mustafa's in Manchester."

"Okay then, come on everyone…"

"Yes, come on time for bed."

"Okay, Mum, see you in the morning."

"Goodnight, Troy."

"Goodnight Athena. Goodnight, love."

SATURDAY

---The Camels Back---

Hestia awoke to the aroma of coffee and burnt toast. As she rolled onto her back, she heard muffled giggles and Athena's voice whisper, "Shhhhh! Be quiet you'll wake her."

"I'm trying to, but Mum will be so surprised," Hope whispered loudly.

Smiling to herself Hestia sat up and propped her pillows behind her and waited for a surprise breakfast.

When Hope crept through her bedroom door, carrying the newspaper followed closely by Athena bearing the breakfast tray, Hestia called loudly, "Good morning koukles!"

They both jumped.

"Oh, Mum, you're supposed to be asleep!" cried Hope disappointedly.

"Told you you'd wake her up!" accused Athena.

"I didn't wake you up did I, Mum?" whined Hope with a frown.

"No, sweetheart, you didn't," said Hestia hugging her, as her youngest daughter threw a look of triumph to her older sister.

"It was the smell of burnt toast," consoled Hestia.

"Tut," said Hope, as she pulled away from the embrace and glared at her mother

"Hope did the toast," sniggered Athena, placing the tray on her mother's knee.

"Oh I see," said Hestia, looking at the scorched and scraped slices set before her. "They are not that bad," she declared as she bravely smothered one in jam under Hope's watchful gaze.

The scorched bread shattered at the first bite, catapulting bits across the tray and the duvet.

Athena burst into laughter, as Hope scowled at her mother.

"You're not eating it properly" she accused. "Take smaller bites," she instructed as if to a naughty child.

"I'll have to. There's only small bits left," whispered Hestia to Athena.

"I heard that," declared Hope with her nose in the air. She laid down on the crumb-strewn duvet and opened the newspaper, pointedly ignoring their laughter.

"Never mind, love. You just need a little more

practice," reassured Hestia, rubbing Hope's back, then hid her grimace as she realised there was now jam all over Hope's pyjama top.

"Fine! Whatever!" stated Hope, still ignoring them.

Athena laughed again and Hope turned another page angrily.

"Well, it was a lovely thought. Thank you, girls. So why are you up so early? It's only 7:45"

"You said we are going to Hamidas this morning, remember, Mum? So I thought you might need to keep up your strength," replied Athena, looking her mother pointedly in the eye.

"Oh God, I'd forgotten," groaned Hestia, remembering the tape and Zak's visit.

"Don't worry about it. We've got lots of time. It's still early, so eat your breakfast. It's far too early to visit yet."

"I can't. I've lost my appetite," moaned Hestia.

"Well, at least drink your coffee," encouraged Athena.

"Don't you want to go to Hamidas?" piped up

Hope from the end of the bed.

Hestia threw a quick look of warning at Athena, before turning to Hope. "Of course I do, but her four boys are very noisy, aren't they?"

Hope nodded vigorously and added, "They are naughty too."

"Well, we'll see what happens today, shall we? Come on, you two, go and get dressed and we'll pop to the supermarket and pick up something nice for Hamida and the boys."

"A chocolate cake!" shouted Hope, bouncing on the bed. "We all like chocolate cake."

"We'll see, now stop jumping, or you'll spill my coffee," warned Hestia.

"Okay," she replied and launched herself into her sister's arms. "Will you get a bath ready for me and find me some clothes?"

"All right, but you'll have to do your teeth while I do that."

"Okay," agreed Hope.

Hestia smiled grimly to herself, as the girls left her alone to drink her coffee. It was good that they were all so close. They'd need each other when she signed those papers. Her cup stopped in mid air, half way to her lips, as she realised what that would mean. God help her, she thought silently, we will all need each other.

Hestia watched as Hope carried the chocolate cake, ever so carefully up the drive of Hamida's house. A startled Hamida answered the door and Hestia felt guilty about their early arrival.

"I know it's early, but we woke up early so we thought we'd bring breakfast," she explained, holding up a bag of croissants while Hope held her cake slightly higher smiling brightly.

"Don't be silly, you are always welcome, no matter how early. Just don't be shocked at the mess," greeted Hamida as she ushered them through the door.

"We came to see you not the house," Hestia assured her. "I'll put the croissants in the oven and you can go get dressed."

"Oh thanks. It might take a while, though. The boys are only half dressed," warned Hamida.

"Take your time, we'll wait for you," said Hestia filling the kettle.

"I'll be as quick as I can," said Hamida, rushing from the room.

"God, she wasn't joking about the mess," whispered Athena, looking at the sink full of pots.

"Don't judge people until you live their lives, sweetheart. It's not easy with four boys and a lazy husband," scolded Hestia gently.

"I know. I didn't mean it like that. Anyway, she chose this life," retorted Athena.

Hestia took a deep breath. She knew she was lecturing again, but she couldn't let her daughter make snap judgements like that.

"Athena, that's not fair. She was only 17 when she got married and then she was pregnant before the year was out. You have a lot to learn about life and relationships. Look, now is not the time for this. Fill the sink and I'll wash up."

"No, you make the coffee and I'll wash up. Hope, get a towel and you can dry."

"No, she won't. Hamida will have no plates left!"

"I'm not that bad! Fine, can I watch sky then?

Sabrina's on soon," said Hope.

"Okay, but I'll call you when the croissants are done," Hestia answered.

Mother and daughter made short work of the chaos in the kitchen and, by the time Hamida herded her boys downstairs, they had breakfast laid out on the table.

"Oh, lovely, Hestia. This is a real treat for me. You should have left the washing up, but thank you anyway, maybe you can do that every morning?" gushed Hamida.

"Hello, Auntie!" shouted the boys one after the other.

"Good morning Adam, Joseph, Yiousef, Ali. Who wants croissants?" asked Hestia. She always addressed them in order of age.

"Me!" Burst out Ali, the youngest and obviously the hungriest of all the boys.

Everyone laughed at his eagerness and love of food.

"Okay sweetheart, do you want cheese or do you want honey?" enquired Hestia with a grin.

"Both!" shouted Ali eagerly.

"Ali!" scolded his mother gently.

"Oops, please Auntie, if that's allowed." Ali quickly glanced at his mother as he replied.

"Of course that's allowed, love. Here you are, go and sit down with Hope in the lounge and take the plate in with you, please."

"Thank you, Auntie," he said, then was gone.

"Well, the rest of you boys are old enough to help yourselves," stated Hamida, as she handed out plates.

When the children were all safely ensconced in the front room, in front of the TV, Athena could wait no longer and asked her first question of many.

"Hamida, just how much Arabic do you know?"

"Well, I understand more than I speak."

"That is the answer we were hoping for," said Athena excitedly.

"Uh oh, that sounds like trouble. What are you two up to?" replied Hamida cautiously.

"Well, we need you to listen to a tape and tell us if you know what is being said."

"What tape? A video tape?" said Hamida, shocked.

"No, it's an audio tape. Look, we found a tape recorder hidden in Mum's chair. None of us put it there, so obviously it must have been dad," Athena said, quietly glancing at the doorway.

"You've got to be joking! What on earth would he do that for?" asked Hamida, amazed.

"Who knows. He thinks he will find out that we are plotting against him or that Mum's having an affair. How are we supposed to know what's going on in his sick head? You know what he's like," hissed Athena.

"Athena, don't exaggerate," warned Hestia.

"I'm not saying anything that's not true."

"Okay, so you want me to listen to a tape that was hidden in Hestia's chair?" Hamida interrupted the spat.

"Well sort of! When we found it, it only had recorded an argument and we thought, if he can use it on us, then we can use it on him. So we decided to hide it in the study and record his conversations but it's all in Arabic. So, we thought of you and here we are," Athena said in a rush.

Hestia sat back in her chair and watched Athena

take out a tiny tape recorder from her handbag, then place it in front of Hamida.

Hamida looked as nervous as Hestia felt, so she tried to reassure her. "Don't worry if you don't understand it. I know you are only learning. It's not important."

"Of course it's important," protested Athena. "He's up to something and I want to know what it is!"

"Athena! Hamida is not going to be pressured in to anything. Now calm down and stop acting so paranoid," Hestia demanded.

"I was only trying to explain," moaned Athena.

"Well, you're not helping," retorted Hestia.

"Now Hamida if you'll listen to the tape and just try your best that's all we can hope for," said Hestia primly.

"I'll do what I can, but don't get your hopes up," replied Hamida.

"That's all we expect," reassured Hestia

Hestia waited as Athena checked the tape then pressed "play."

"*Ya habibi. Kif Halak. Ana koueish al*

hamdourilha!............." Zak's voice sounded out deep and clear.

There was a pause while Zak awaited the caller's answer. Athena pressed the "pause" button and looked expectantly at Hamida.

"That's easy. He said, "Hi how are you?" Hamida said, sheepishly, not looking at anyone in particular.

Hestia sat down close to Hamida and touched her arm, making her turn to face her.

"I know. "Habibi" means *love,* so please feel free to tell me whatever you heard. I understood very little, but it was obvious he was talking to another woman. I'm prepared for the worst."

"Okay, but just remember I'm only repeating what Zak's saying," Hamida replied looking uncomfortable. She released the "pause" button and Zak's voice broke the uneasy silence.

"Great! So you'll catch the 6:20 flight from Benghazi and arrive at Heathrow at about 11.00 and then Mustafa and I will meet you at arrivals. Just wait and we'll find you. Don't wonder around and get lost.

I'd hate to loose you, now that I've found you."

His rich laughter flowed deeply from the Dictaphone and, although Hestia didn't understand the words he said, she knew their meaning simply by the sound of self-amusement.

Hamida paused the tape and asked for a pen and paper, rewound it and listened again whilst taking notes. When she finished, she looked at Hestia and asked,

"Are you sure you want to hear this? What will you get out of all this?"

Hestia said calmly, "Just tell me what he's up to, I need to know."

"Fine," Hamida replied resignedly. "First of all it sounds as though he's checking times of flights from Benghazi to Heathrow, then he's arranging to pick that person up." Hamida said this, still looking at the notes she wrote down. She reached to turn the tape back on, but Hestia spoke up. "Is that all? It sounded much longer."

"That's all I understood" Hamida said quickly, too quickly, but Hestia decided to hold her council until the end of the tape.

After a short pause, they heard Zak say,

"I can't wait to see you arousa! One more night alone and then we'll be together. See you tomorrow. I love you."

There was a firm click as he replaced the receiver in its cradle and they all stared at the Dictaphone when they heard Zak utter a series of expletives quietly to himself.

Hestia schooled her features as best as she could. She knew the meaning of that last sentence and so she should. How many times had her husband called her "his new bride" during their first blissful months of marriage? Too many to count! The words "I love you" had drips from his lips every time he needed her or every time he needed something from her.

Hamida cleared her throat and glanced at Hestia, but never quite met her eyes. "I.... I didn't catch all of that ... I didn't understand most of it, stuttered Hamida.

"Well, I did!" stated Hestia firmly looking directly at Hamida who had the grace to blush.

"Were you ever going to tell me or were you all thinking I'd never find out? I may be naïve and trusting, but I am not stupid!" She retorted harshly.

"I am sorry. I am so sorry, I wanted to tell you. Mustafa and I had an almighty row about the whole thing. I only found out that she was coming on Thursday and I told Zak not to bring her round here, and that's when Mustafa started shouting and all hell broke loose, he hit me on my back and told me not to disrespecting him." she blurted out in a rush as tears of regret welled in her eyes.

"Who exactly is she?" asked Hestia carefully.

"Semira," said Hamida miserably. "Mustafa came back from Zak's flat about a month ago in a black mood. He wouldn't talk about what caused it, all week, then when we were watching TV one night, he came out and told me that Zak had gone back to Libya to get married. I couldn't believe it! Mustafa said neither could he. He had tried to tell Zak not to be stupid and that he should try to save his marriage, not get into another one with someone he doesn't know. But Zak wouldn't listen to him. I really wanted to tell you." She paused. "I feel so guilty."

Hestia stared at her sister-in-law. She was

speechless. So this is what he was doing. Not only was he breaking every vow he had ever made to her, he had now made those same vows to another woman. A woman who lived far enough away not to know what sort of man he was. But what really hurt her the most was the fact that he obviously had given up on their marriage and not bothered to inform her! What was he doing? Keeping his options open? If it didn't work out with the new model he always had the old one to go back to?

Well, wait until he does receive those divorce papers back, she thought to herself, with her signature signed on every page! Let him have his new wife, because he would never have her again. Never will she let him walk all over her. If this was the end of their marriage she was damn sure she was going to get as much out of it as she could!

    Hestia became aware, through her haze of indignation of raised voices. Athena was giving rest to her outrage over her father's duplicity.

    "Why didn't you tell us?" she stormed .

    "I've told you! It's not as simple as you make it

sound. Please don't be angry with me," pleaded Hamida.

"Angry? You have no idea how angry I am!" Athena roared.

"You're my auntie! Family! You've taken his side against us! How am I supposed to feel?"

"It's not like that!" retorted Hamida desperately.

Hestia knew she should reprimand Athena, but she couldn't bring herself to speak out. After all, Athena was saying everything she herself wanted to say.

She wanted to stand before Hamida and rage at her and say all those same things Athena was saying. "How can he marry someone else? Sorry! All ready be *married* to someone else. He is a bigamist! That's what he is, *a bigamist*!! He 's a fucking bigamist."

"Not under Islamic law, as long as you love all the women equally". argued Hamida kindly

"Sod the fucking Islamic law! We live in England, Islamic law doesn't count here. If Muslims want to go by Islamic law then they should go back to their countries and live under their rules and regulations there. Not here! Can I wife marry as many men as she wants then?" spat Athena "How many things has that bastard done, and condoned it all, by saying that it was all okay because the "Koran says so!?" Well, no more. This time he has gone too far. As far as we're concerned, he is not our father. If I never see him again it will be too soon!" Athena shouted as tears streamed down her face.

Hestia watched her daughter towering over her auntie and smiled inwardly. Hamida was 6ft tall while Athena stood 5'5" in her stocking feet. Only now Athena stood looking down at her disconsolate aunt sat hunched in her chair. Athena's words condemned her father, but her tears belied the fact that her feelings were not as removed as she would like to have everyone believe.

While Athena became more and more agitated, Hestia decided to call a halt to the argument, not for Hamidas benefit, but for her daughters, who's control was clearly slipping.

"Athena come here!" ordered Hestia.

"But Mum, you can't just take this lying down. You must have something to say to her!" replied Athena.

"I do and if you stop shouting for two minutes, I might be able to do just that!" said her mother slowly and calmly.

Athena looked at her mother trying to decide to do as she asked or fight for her rights to say her piece. Her obedience to her mother made her take a chair albeit with a huff.

"I understand why you didn't tell me, Hamida, and I don't want to have a fall out with you about this. But I want you to tell me, is there anything else I ought to know?" asked Hestia.

Hamida hesitated slightly before looking Hestia in the eye and then saying, "Well…actually… Zak and Mustafa have gone to Heathrow to … meet Semira. Then they are…bringing her back here. They should be here by…3 pm."

Hestia sat as still as possible. She felt as though the slightest movement would shatter emotionally her into a thousand shards, like glass of the windscreen she crashed through years earlier during an argument with Zak. Slowly, she flexed her toes, then her fingers. Gradually feeling came back to her limbs, enough for her to reach for her cup of coffee. Cold though it was, she needed something normal, ordinary, to do to keep reality within reach.

"I'm sorry if this hurts Hestia, but you wanted the truth."

"No, no, you…are quite right. It's just that I didn't realise that he…would bring her…where I live, where our children live. We might pass each other on the street and never realise," said Hestia in disbelief.

"That's because you'll only be able to see her fucking eyeballs and nothing else. The rest will be covered in a sheet," griped Athena.

Hamida tutted as she had taken to wearing robes as soon as she had married.

"Athena, stop it!" snapped Hestia who's patience was wearing thin.

"Well he won't be making the same mistakes again, will he? He'll make sure she's a proper Muslim wife, not like you mum, you obviously let him down and so did the rest of us." Athena bitched.

"If all you can do is be nasty about a woman you have never met, then you can go and sit with the rest of the children!" Hestia threatened.

Athena glared at her mother, but she held her tongue and gathered the breakfast things and began to clear them away.

Hamida started to rise to help, but Hestia's hand on her palm stayed her.

"No let her work it off," explained Hestia.

"Well, if you are sure," said Hamida worryingly.

"I am," assured Hestia with a tight smile.

So, as Athena tidied with a vengeance, the sisters-in-law sat opposite each other and came to terms with the events that had taken place earlier that morning.

"I'm not being awful, Hestia, but its one o'clock and I have a lot of things to do before Mustafa gets back," apologised Hamida.

"Oh, of course, don't worry. I'll make a move, but I meant it, I do not want…this to change our friendship. We have things to do before the shops close anyway. Athena, go and tell your sister it's time to go, please."

As Athena left the room, Hestia faced Hamida.

"Will you do me a last favour…only if it's

possible." "Okay, if I can," said Hamida consciously.

"I want to see her. Not to say anything, just to see what kind of person she is. Look, don't say no. If the opportunity arises, then please let me know. She doesn't have to know who I am. You can say I am a friend. It wouldn't be a lie. I would like to think we still are."

"Of course we are still friends and I'm really sorry about all this, but I can't promise anything. I don't even know the woman," said Hamida.

"Just try please. I'll leave it at that," said Hestia, as she squeezed her hand and smiled. She then put all evidence of her discoveries away, until it was impossible to tell that they had visited.

As Athena helped Hope fit her seatbelt, Hestia bid Hamida goodbye and reminded her of her promise. Soon they were making their way home, Hope chattering constantly about her cousins and the things they said and did, most of which they weren't supposed to do.

As they pulled into the driveway, Troy opened the front door and picked Hope up, then kissed her hello.

He repeated this for his mum and his sister before

putting the kettle on and sitting down at the dinning table to hear the results of Hamida's translation.

His first indication that it was bad news was Athena's stony silence, pronounced flounce onto a chair beside him and arms firmly folded across her chest.

"Well? What was said?" he asked when his sister made it obvious that she wasn't going to say anything.

"Wait until I put Hope's TV on upstairs, then we can speak privately" said his mum.

By the time Hestia sat down at the table, Troy had made them all tea and biscuits. Hestia hoped the whole belief about tea's calming effects was true, as Troy was as bad as his sister, once he was angered.

Athena still sat in silence, stewing over what she had learned earlier that morning.

"Well? Is someone going to tell me what is going on? Is it that bad?" asked Troy, exasperated.

"Of course I am, love, but it's not good news, so don't start getting upset or angry. It was bad enough Athena started shouting at Hamida," Hestia said, with a sigh.

"Well, what did you expect me to do? She should have told us! She is our aunt and she is supposed to be our friend! Some friend she is!" Snapped Athena at her mum.

"She's still my friend!" said Hestia firmly. "She only found out on Thursday, then we came round a day later and she didn't know what to say without hurting anyone. Anyway, she told us in the end, so stop sulking," chided Hestia, with a frown.

"Well, I think she should have told us straight away," accused Athena.

"Shut up or leave the table!" demanded Hestia.

Troy stared at his mother, shocked at the speed she lost her temper.

He then glanced at his sister as she looked thunderous and not in the least chastised. Unwilling to ask either of them about the tape, he waited.

When it seemed he would have to repeat his question, his mother said, "I'm going to tell you what happened with the tape, but don't act like your sister or I won't say another word," Hestia warned, looking at his sister who threw a mutinous look back at their mother.

Troy decided to keep silent and simply nodded.

"Good. Well you know your dad wants a divorce?" she asked Troy, who nodded again.

"He wanted one for a reason. He got married again, to a Libyan woman," Hestia stated flatly.

"He…he…can't have. He's still married to you." declared Troy, astounded.

"According to Islamic law, you can marry as many wives as you want!" spat Athena.

"But…he can't have…when? Where?" asked Troy.

As Athena opened her mouth for her next attack, Hestia jumped in saying, "Remember when we never saw him for a week or so last month? Well, it must've been then. He must've gone over to Libya and married her then," she said, with an obvious tremor.

"I can't believe he has done this," Troy said more to himself than anyone else in the room. "Is he going to go back to Libya?" demanded Troy.

"Oh no, he's not going there. She is coming here!" replied Athena spitefully.

"What? Come again, sis!" shouted Troy

"Calm down!" ordered Hestia. "If you ll listen, I'll tell you exactly what's happening at Hamida's."

Troy started to speak, but Hestia held up her hand. He waited for her to speak.

"Do you want to hear this or what? I'm not going to talk over you!"

Hestia looked Troy in the eye and waited for his answer.

"Fine, but don't leave anything out!"

"Hamida translated the tape, as much as she could, stating that it started with Zak talking to someone he called *habibi,* which meant *love*. So it was obvious a woman he was intimate with. Then, he made arrangements to pick her up from Heathrow. Today!" Hestia said, slowly.

Troy sat and stared at his mother in disbelief.

"That's not the best bit!" cried Athena. "Oh no. Hamida knew all about this other woman! But did she tell Mum? Did she hell?"

"Athena will you stop being childish please!" shouted Hestia, her patience snapping.

"I'm sick of having to referee this whole family.

Can't you think of anyone else except yourself? Is it all about how you feel? I'm the one who he's done this too! Not you, or you! It's me he wants to hurt. Well, he has. After all these years and the crap I have put up with, he's the one to walk away from me. That hurts me, but it doesn't kill me. I m still alive! I'm still breathing and by God, I'm going to keep breathing and if he wants to divorce me and start again, then I'm not going to stop him. Give me those divorce papers, I ve put up with his lies, his other women, the affairs, the moods, the violence, the emotional scars, I am ready to move on now" Hestia hissed at Athena.

"Now mum don't get over excited, you know Athena's got a temper. She speaks from her heart and not her head," cajoled Troy placing one hand on his Mum's shoulder.

"Over excited? Is that what you think I am? Don't be so patronizing!" she shouted, shrugging Troy's hand away. "I'm just finally making a decision I should have made years ago, why did I put up with all these things, why did I suffer in silence? I did it for you, for my children, I saw my parents divorcing when I was little and I vowed never to let my marriage go, I vowed to be happy, to sacrifice everything for my children, that's why I am still here, with him." she stated more calmly, holding out her hand for the papers Athena passed to her with a gleeful look in her eyes.

Hestia whipped out the papers and signed them all without looking at any of the pages again. She knew what they said, but she couldn't care less about any of the accusations he made. She had made a decision and she was going to do it quickly, before she talked herself out if it.

Athena and Troy shared a look of disbelief. Although she signed the papers and stuffed them in the reply envelope, neither one thought she would post them and that was until she stood up and shouted to Hope to get her shoes and coat on because they were going to town.

"Mum where are you going?" asked Athena worried.

"I'm going to post this letter, then put the house on the market," replied her mother with a determined air.

"The house?" squeaked Athena.

"But where are we going to go? Mum, don't be too hasty. We have to think about this!"

"I'm sick of thinking. That's all I've done for months. Now it's time for action. If your father is making a new life, I'm not going to cling to the old one. There you are! Hope! Go and get your shoes on love, we are going to town. Athena if you are coming, I don't want any arguments. What I am going to do is not open to discussion, is that understood?" stated Hestia to her two eldest children.

"Of course I'm coming along, but are you sure, Mum?" Athena asked.

"Yes!" stated Hestia firmly.

"I'd like to go too, Mum, but I've got an interview in an hour," said Troy reliantly.

"Oh, love, you never told me," said Hestia, concerned "What's wrong with the garage where you are at the moment?"

"Nothing," assured Troy "But there is no chance of promotion, Mum. But if I can get in at this new job, there's a chance of a management opening."

"Okay then, good luck, sweetheart. Will you be in for tea?" asked Hestia.

"I don't know, Mum. I'll phone and let you know," he said, following his mum to the front door, then waving them both off.

Hope did most of the talking during the drive to town and then happily skipped up to the post box and posted the large envelope that would change all their lives forever while Athena and her mother silently looked on.

Athena thought her mum looked a little pale as they headed for the real estate agent's office, so, when Hope whispered her need for the toilet yet again, Athena jumped in and suggested they stop for some tea and coffee, which Hope clapped her hands and her mum nearly nodded and smiled.

Athena tried to provide small talk, so Hope wouldn't pick up on her mother's dark mood, but, by the time they finished their snack, even Hope was looking askance at Hestia. Athena reached across the table and took her mother's clenched hand in hers asking, "Are you okay with this, Mum? You know it was a sudden decision and that it doesn't have to be done today."

"Yes I do, sweetheart," said Hestia, as she squeezed her daughter's hand, straightened her shoulders and took a fortifying breath. "But, if I don't do this now, I know I won't have the strength tomorrow or the next day or the next. I need my own home somewhere, mine, not his, where I can lock the door and know to be alone! To be safe and calm. Somewhere I can make a home for my children, especially Hope," declared Hestia softly, giving Hope a hug.

"Now come on," Hesita continued, firmly. She stood. "I've got to find out how much we can expect to get after all the costs, divide it in half, then I'll know how much I'll have to put down as a deposit for our home. Our home, girls. Just imagine, a house full of Katti's girls!" Hestia whispered theatrically hugging her daughters hard, making them groan and giggle.

It was after 7 p.m., by the time they all returned home, dumping armfuls of papers on the dining table. Athena pressed "play" on the answering machine whilst reaching around the corner to flick the stove on to warm the kettle.

The first was Troy, letting them know he was spending the night with Vickie again. This is becoming a habit, Athena thought to herself, smiling. The second call was from Hamida. She had left a message saying she had tried to contact Hestia on her mobile.

"Mum? Hamida said, she's tried to phone you on your mobile. Has she actually phoned you?"

"I don't think so. I didn't hear the mobile ring at all today."

"Where is your mobile, Mum?"

"In my bag. I think it's in the car, love."

Athena brought Hestia's bag inside. As she looked through the bag, she found the mobile phone. She looked at the screen. "Mum, you have five missed calls and a message! It's been on silent all day, no wonder the phone never rang." Athena waited no more as she dialled 901 to retrieve the message Hamida had left.

"Hi, Hestia. Look, it's only me" she said quietly, so quietly that Athena had to turn up the volume "She's here. I've been trying to get through to you all afternoon, so I thought I'd leave a message. Listen, Zak asked if I could take Semira back home to his flat at 7.30, so I said, yes. But, if you want to meet her, phone me back by 7 and I 'll go by the petrol station and you can be there. Accidentally of course. You can come over and say hi and I'll introduce you as Zak's wife. You've got to act surprised and upset as if you've just found out. I know you are, of course, but…well…you understand. Look, phone me back on my mobile, not at home. I hate all this lying, but I wouldn't do this for anyone else, you know that, right? Okay, enough said. I've got to go. A woman can only spend so much time on the loo! Speak to you soon. Take care, bye."

Hamida 's voice whispered loudly and, just before she was disconnected, Athena could hear her flush the toilet and smiled humourlessly at the picture it painted in her mind's eye.

Athena put her finger on the "delete" button, hesitated, and then drew back her hand reluctantly.

"Go on, press it!" said Hestia loudly, from behind Athena, making her jump wildly and utter an expletive that made her mother do a double take.

"Don't do that!" Athena shouted to her mother,

pressing a hand to her chest. "I nearly had a heart attack! God!"

"Well you were going to delete a message meant for me! It serves you right," her mother defended herself.

"I thought about it, but I didn't do it! It's not a good idea! Anyway it's 7:15 now, so it's too late." She smiled at her mother.

"We'll see about that," said Hestia, dialling Hamida's mobile number.

"Hello?" came Hamida's voice, loud and clear.

"Hi, Hamida it's me, can you talk?" asked Hestia quietly.

"Oh, hi! No of course not!" she replied loudly, making it clear that this was going to be a strange conversation.

"Okay, no problem," said Hestia "I'll talk and you answer as best as you can, okay? Now, are you still at home?"

"Yes, yes we are all fine," came the reply. "Good. Is it okay to meet at the BP Petrol station in Wynyard?"

"Oh yes, that would be fantastic. Yes that's not a problem".

"Shall we say in about 15 minutes?" asked Hestia.

" No, you cook the chicken for at least 30 minutes, possibly 35!"

"Okay, thanks Hamida. I'll be there.

"Okay then see you soon take care, Bye fr now," responded Hamida, pretending to give her brother some cooking advice.

"Right, we've got to be at BP in half an hour," Hestia told Athena. "Don't start with the back chat", she continued, holding up a hand to stop her daughter's next words. "I'm going. If you don't want to come. I'll understand."

Athena couldn't help herself, so she looked at Hestia and said, "I was going to say, if you are going through with this, then I' m coming with you. Anyway I want to see what she looks like, see if she's wearing a table cloth on her head," muttered Athena.

"I'm definitely not taking you with that attitude! We have got to pretend that we have just bumped into

Hamida by accident. Then, she will introduce us and say that I'm Zak's wife. If all goes as planned, I get to tell her exactly what kind of person Zak is and Hamida won't get into trouble as we met by accident in the petrol station," explained Hestia.

"Fine, I can do that. I'm just so bloody annoyed that he has done this to you," said Athena heatedly. "But I just want to see her too. I won't even get out of the car," she promised.

"Okay," relented Hestia, as she sat down. "Oh God, I've just had a thought. What if she doesn't speak English?" Hestia paused.

"Come, it's time to go. We'll find out in 15 minutes, I suppose," said Athena, pulling her mum to her feet and pushing her out the door.

"Come on, squirt, we have got to go and get some petrol," Athena shouted upstairs to her little sister.

"Coming!" came the reply, followed by the sound of thundering footsteps flying down the stairs.

"Wow! You make a lot of noise for a little squirt," joked Athena.

"You make a lot of noise for a big squirt!" Hope

threw the words over her shoulder as she climbed into the back seat.

"Oohh, listen you?" Athena laughed, mimicking her best friend, Sara.

"Belt up!" she ordered, then stuck out her tongue at her little sister in the rear view mirror.

"Oi, you are not supposed to say that!" shouted Hope, giggling.

"What belt up?" asked Athena smiling.

"Oi, Mum, tell her!" demanded Hope.

But Hestia never heard a word of the exchange. Her mind was on what she was going to say when finally face to face with Semira, if she could even understand what would be said.

At 7:31 p.m., Athena parked the car in an empty space at the side of the building, and then they waited.

It was a full six minutes before Athena spotted Hamida's car pulling into the petrol station. It stopped in front of the pumps. After a smile of encouragement from her daughter, Hestia climbed out the car and walked over to Hamidas who was sat talking to Semira. As she walked towards the car Hestia slowed down, in order to study the woman sitting in the passenger's side at her friend's car.

All an all she was a remarkable creature. She was about 35-year-old, which was a slight surprise as Hestia was expecting to see a younger, more impressionable woman than the one before her. Her features were plain and serious, but not unpleasant. She smiled at something Hamida was explaining and Hestia was amazed at the transformation. She was lovely. Her whole face lit up, making her dark eyes sparkle and Hestia now knew what Zak saw when he looked at her; he could never resist a pretty face. Realizing she was approaching from the passenger's side, Hestia hesitated a step away, unsure if she should knock on the window and be that close to Semira.

That decision was taken out of her hands as the woman in question turned and looked enquiringly at her.

Hestia quickly glanced away towards Hamida, who gave her an unbelievably bright smile, but she could only nester a sickly grin in return.

Her sister-in-law must have told Semira to roll down the window, and Hestia realized she had no idea what she would say to this woman who looked so much like herself.

"Hi Hestia! How are you? What a coincidence seeing you here!" Hamida practically shouted.

"Oh, hi, Hamida. My daughters and I just filled up," said Hestia bending down, then leaning her forearms on the window, trying to act nonchalant. "How are you?"

"Oh fine, we're all doing fine," Hamida replied nervously. "This is my new friend, Semira," she continued quickly before she lost her nerve.

"Hello, how do you do?" said Zak's second wife, in a low, well-modulated voice as she held out her hand in greeting.

Hestia took the proffered hand and gave a slightly too firm shake in an effort to overcompensate for nerves.

"I'm very pleased to meet you, Semira," she replied politely, trying not to let her voice choke her. "It's always nice to meet a new friend of my sister-in-law's."

Semira looked surprised and gave a delightful

smile to Hestia. "But, I'm also a sister-in-law to Hamida. Does that not make us also sisters-in-law?" she asked hopefully.

Every cell in Hestia's body screamed, not to say what she knew she must. She almost gave in to the temptation of lying and let the woman believe what she wanted to. But, she knew if she walked away now, this poor woman would probably end up learning about Zak the hard way.

Hestia had "been there, done that" and knew deep down inside that this woman was innocent of Zak's plans and, most importantly, the truth. "Well I suppose so. I'm Zak's wife, have you met him yet? I didn't realize that Haled had married again. Congratulations." guessed Hestia, hating herself, but hating Zak even more for putting them in this situation. "You are Zak's wife?" Semira practically whispered. "But…you…can't be. You mean…you used to…to be his wife? He is divorced. She declared trying to persuade Hestia to agree.

"No. I 'm still married to Zak," Hestia said, smiling hard. "I think Haled must have been mistaken when he told you."

"No…Haled…didn't tell me, I have only just…met him today. Zak told me, I am Zak's wife, we got married last month," Semira rushed on, her voice getting louder and higher. "He told me weeks ago, when we first met. He told he'd been divorced for years. His wife wasn't able to live like a good Muslim woman should. He said she had affairs, drank and smoked. He divorced her years ago. You are lying! He's my husband! He married me! Not you!"

The woman was getting hysterical, Hestia realized, but she had to go on, she had to do this.

"Are you telling me that Zak Kattis is married to you?" Hestia asked letting some anger she felt show.

"Yes!" Semira declared unsure of herself.

"Well, I am sorry to tell you that he has been married to me for the last 23 years! We have never been divorced!" said Hestia forcefully needing to make her point clear. "If he told you otherwise, then I'm not surprised. He'll tell you anything to get his own way!"

"You are lying!" repeated Semira "She's lying, tell her Hamida. Why is she saying that?" pleaded Semira.

"Well…I'm sorry, Semira…it's true…" Hamida said sadly. "I wanted to tell you. I wanted to tell you both…but…Mustafa made me promise…not to. He said it was Zak's business and it was not my place to interfere!" She ended miserably, grasping the hand of the now tearful woman who sat next to her.

"But…it's not true! Please! It's not true!" she begged. "Zak told me his wife left him, took everything they had, left him with nothing and he was so happy to have met me and be together, this is not true".

"I wish it wasn't, but as far as British law is concerned, Zak can only have one wife and that is my right as long as I'm married to him," stated Hestia.

"British Law? What about Muslim Law? I'm as much his wife as you are! If not more! You are his old wife. You gave him children, but now he wants me. I'm younger and prettier. I'm the type of wife he wants, the type you could never be for him! If he was so happy with you why did he go thousands of miles to find me? I'm going to make him the happiest man alive!" His new wife declared fighting back with the only weapon left to her.

Hestia said angrily and her temper getting the better of her, "You can try all you like to make him happy, but think about this, is he going to make you happy? This "wonderful" husband you have tried to cling to, who got you to marry him, if he's lied about having another wife, a son and two daughters, what else isn't he telling you?"

"It's not true!" Semira repeated more to herself than anyone else.

"Semira, I'm sorry you had to find out like this…it should have been Zak who would tell you all this," Hestia said softly.

"I think I should take her home," said Hamida, when it became obvious Semira hadn't heard a word and was quietly crying into her hands. Then, she added, "God I could kill him for this, this has to be the worst thing he's done to date!"

"Okay…I'm sorry…Hamida I never wanted this to involve you…but it's over now! Semira…Semira!" Hestia said loudly, making the woman look at her over the fingertips. "I didn't tell you this to hurt you. Zak has been my husband for much longer than he has yours

I…know him…I know what he is capable of! This is an awful thing he has done to you, to me and his children," said Hestia, looking pointedly at the girls in her own car.

Semira followed her gaze and hung her head as she realised she was the focus of their attention.

"I want to go home…please, I want to go back to Libya, I have nothing here, I thought I would have a future, a happy life with Zak and look at what's happening..." she said to Hamida, ignoring all that Hestia had said.

"I meant it Semira! I don't want you to think I wanted to hurt you! You need to know that Zak has already got a wife and three beautiful children. If he has lied to you…then…well…you need to ask him why."

"I really want to go home, Hamida," Semira repeated again, ignoring Hestia's words of apology.

"Okay…I'll speak with you later Hestia," said her sister-in-law with a sad smile.

Hestia was still staring after the car as it rounded the curve and disappeared from site. Only when the horn blared from behind her did she realise she stood in the forecourt, blocking the exit of several cars. Her legs shook with shock as she hurried back to her car.

Later that night, long after Hope was in bed and Athena had given up trying to get details of the conversation from her mother did Hestia finally relax enough to allow herself to relive the last 12 hours that seemed more like an eternity.

The fact that her suspicions had been confirmed by the translation of the tape was not a big surprise, but to find out the other woman was another wife was a massive one. Having to confront this woman with the truth, and lies, of her marriage was even more of a trial—one of the hardest ones of her life, a life so crammed, with bad days, hard times and broken dreams that for this day to be classed as a *trial* was quite an achievement, even by Zak's standards.

Hysterical laughter threatened to bubble up and was forced quickly down as the phone rang, making Hestia run to check the ID of the caller.

Only because she recognised Hamida's mobile number did she even consider answering the late call.

"Hello?" Hestia asked.

"Hestia, it's me," whispered Hamida tearfully.

"I'm just letting you know what has been happening at this end."

"What's wrong? Are you crying?"

"I'm okay, just upset because Mustafa and I have had a row again."

"Oh, Hamida, is this because of today? I'm really sorry you had to get involved. I wish I could have done this without you, but I'm glad I did it. I had to see her and I'm not sorry I told her about Zak. Did she say anything after you had gone?"

"No, not a word. She was so upset, but I think it was mostly with herself and Zak. He had lied to her and she believed him. She had no reason not to believe him. No one likes to be made a fool of."

"So why did you argue with Mustafa?"

"Zak phoned about an hour ago. Semira told him that we met you and the things that were said. Zak and Semira had a row, so he phoned Mustafa and had a go about me. Mustafa took my side and told him to sort out his own wives and he'll sort out his. Then Mustafa started having an argument with me. He wanted to know why I even talk to you. I told him how we *accidentally* met and that you came over to me. Of course I wasn't going to ignore you or lie to you, but I didn't tell you or Semira who either one was. It just happened!"

"Did he believe you?"

"Not really, but he didn't call me a liar out-right, but he made it obvious about what he thought. Anyway, I just wanted to let you know…that Zak knows, so don't be surprised if he calls or if he visits," she warned with a sniffle.

"I won't be…and thank you. You have been a good friend about all this."

"Come on Hestia, what are sisters for, if they don't stick up for each other? Just promise me that all this means that you are going to make a clean break!"

"It does. It's so clean, that I have put the house on the market this afternoon and, by all accounts, it should be snapped up within a week. There is actually a waiting list to buy houses in this estate."

"Really? Wow, I can't believe you have actually done it. You are so brave, Hestia. Does Zak know you are selling the house?"

"Yes he does, but I can't see it being a problem

now. I know he needs the money and he can't complain about my behaviour after today. If you are dealing out praise, then I'd better let you know about the rest of my news," teased Hestia.

"Well go on then," urged Hamida, when she got no answer.

"Are you sitting down?"

"Actually I'm on the loo, not doing anything. It's the only place I can go where I'm guaranteed to be alone," giggled Hamida.

"I got the divorce papers from Zak's solicitor on Thursday. I was really devastated at first, but after what happened today, I signed them, then went out and posted them."

"You are joking," whispered Hamida, obviously amazed.

"I'm not joking, Hamida. This is the end of it! I have had enough! I have been a failure all my life, I have been weak, but he has given up on everything, then what's the point in trying? What am I holding on to? I ve been unhappy for years, I ve been let down by Zak for years, I ve been put down for years but Hamida I finally realised that I have my children and that's all that matters to me now!"

"Wow, I wish I was more like you, Hestia! I wish I could be stronger to take the first step. Sometimes I see my life and I think what a waste its been. Unable to see the world, unable to go anywhere, unable to interact with people, unable to communicate, be free. I was talking to Zain and she said the same thing. What is the matter with men?"

"I have had this for over 20 years Hamida but over the last few years its been hell. Its all in the name of Allah, all in the name of the Koran, but I just think he uses his religion to make himself look better. I hope things work out for you but it looks like you too are heading for disaster. You have only been married for less than ten years who knows things may change for the better". said Hestia.

"Thanks, I'll try to hang in there, but my patience is wearing thin too." replied Hamida.

"Look, thanks for phoning. You have put things in perspective for me. I was feeling a little sorry for myself before you called, now, well, I feel a lot easier about what's happened."

"That's okay, Hestia, any time. I have got to go now. Mustafa has just come back. Phone me if you need anything…I mean it…anything…any time!"

"I will and thank you again, you are an angel," said Hestia emotionally. "Bye."

"Bye, Hestia," replied Hamida, sniffling again.

Hestia stood up smiling to herself. She really did feel better. More in control of herself and her life than she had for a long time.

As she climbed into bed, a few minutes later the only thoughts that filled her head were of the future.

A future that looked a lot brighter that it had an hour ago.

SUNDAY

--- The Move ---

It was a bright shaft of sunlight laying across Hestia's pillow that woke her up earlier than usual.

She lay still, squinting and wondering what was wrong with her curtains. Sitting upright with a start, she looked at her bare windows then at the multitude of boxes stacked with precision against bare walls.

Moving Day! How could she have forgotten? Even for a moment? Glancing at the bedside table for her clock and encountering nothing but space, she dug under the pillow for her mobile phone. 6:52 am. The van would not arrive 'until after 9:00 a.m., so there was no rush to rise. Hestia settled down until Hope decided to make her appearance.

I can't believe this is the last day I'll ever wake up in this house, Hestia thought to herself, not only because she had grown attached to it, but after the commotion that her discussion with Semira had caused, Zak had arrived with an axe to grind. She remembered as Zak arrived full of hell and fury, giving everyone the evil eye and ordering his children upstairs. She relayed the conversation in her head.

Hope was already half way there, but both Troy and Athena stayed seated on the sofa, looking their father in the eye.

"If you want to discuss your illegal marriage, you can do it in front of us," declared Athena calmly.

She and Troy had talked at some length about what they could do when their father came, knowing that his coming to the house was guaranteed. They agreed that, no matter what, they would stay calm and not leave their mother alone with him.

"Athena!" said her mother shocked, not at what she had said, but more that she actually dared to say it to her father's face.

"What have you been telling them?" Zak spat at Hestia.

"Don't you dare blame Mum! I was there when we bumped into your *new bride*!" Said Athena remaining calm but squeezing in a little bit extra.

"I told you to get out, you re not my fucking daughter! I want to talk with her!" he shouted to Athena and Troy, indicating his words to Hestia.

"If you have anything to say, then say it to the

whole family!" Troy said firmly.

"Troy, its okay. Go upstairs and you, as well, Athena," rushed Hestia, forever the peacemaker.

"No thank you, Mum. We are both staying!" she replied.

"Fine!" said Zak as he walked to the other end of the room, then sat with his back to them at the dinning table.

Hestia looked at her children, raising her eyebrows in silent enquiry, but all she received were angelic smiles and hard eyes. Holding back a sigh, she turned and walked to sit opposite Zak.

"What did you think you were doing? Do you listen to your husband or Hamida?" hissed Zak as soon as she sat down.

"Neither. You're not worth the bother! I never knew you would become a bigamist until I met your other wife. What did you think you were doing Zak?" Hestia shot back furious at his accuracy.

Zak stared in amazement at Hestia's flushed face. "Bigamist? What's that?"

"It's illegal to be married to two people at the

same time, in civilised countries!" she stated heatedly, wondering to herself, if she dared to use this to her advantage.

"I am only married to her under Islamic law, so I m not breaking any laws," said Zak with a self satisfied smile.

"Maybe not, but you have definitely committed adultery! Remember that? When we get divorced, it won't be based on the lies you filled those papers in. I'll make the terms because I have witnesses." said Hestia slowly.

"What witnesses? Your own kids? The kids that have no name?' Zak started to laugh. 'The kids that are a failure? Ha ha! You re so funny Hestia. There is no one that's a reliable witness. No proof!" Again that smirk.

"I don't mean family! Look, you want a divorce and you'll get it, but we are going to get half of everything!"

"What makes you think you deserve half of everything that's mine?" he said with an urge, knowing he was looking for a response.

Hestia chose her words carefully. "Its not yours, Zak. It's ours! If you spent more time being with your family, you would not have lost anything. It's always been you first, and then the rest of us last. Well, I've had enough! I have had to put the house up for sale and we are going to split the profits in half!"

"I'm the one who worked hard to pay for the house. It's in my name. What makes you think you ll be legally entitled to have any part of this house?" he sneered.

"Wrong again, Zak! I have consulted a solicitor and, as the house is in joint names, and, as the children are to stay with me, I'm actually entitled to three-quarters of the profits. But…" Hestia jumped in as Zak tried to object. "But as long as you co-operate, I'll only take half!"

"Only half? That's rich!" he roared.

"I can make this happen. I only want what's fair, but if you push me, I'll take you for all I can get!" she warned.

"All you can get? I don't have anything for you to take, so don't threaten me!"

"Don't threaten you? Why not? That's all you have done to us for years!" Hestia shouted. "Think long and hard before you make a decision, Zak, if you want half. I'm willing to share, but if you want to fight, just know that you'll lose, Zak! I have covered everything!" She said with certainty.

"You always were a sly cow. I could never trust you! You brought your children up the way you wanted them to be brought up, with no manners, no respect, they are rude, useless and they will never make it on their own Hestia, because they will never have my blessing."

"You can insult me all you want, but the facts remain the same! You have got your new wife, you are getting a divorce and this house is to be sold and I'm taking half," Hestia said bitterly.

"Fine, do it!" he said jumping to his feet, but then so did Athena, followed by Troy.

"Get what you can but do it quickly!" he greeted as he walked through the door.

"Well! That went well!" sighed Athena, then giggled at the incredulous looks from the other two.

Sounds of movement from the direction of

Hope's bedroom halted Hestia's reminiscence. Looking at her mobile, that showed 8:15 a.m., made Hestia softly swear, then jump out of bed. Grabbing her dressing gown, she headed down the corridor to rouse Athena and Troy.

After the initial panic, everyone managed to get dressed, eat breakfast and still have ten minutes to spare before the van arrived.

"Well, Mum, are you sad to leave?" asked Athena over the rim of her coffee cup.

Hestia smiled softly. "Yes, I am actually. It's not exactly been a happy home, but it's my first house that I owned in England. Hope was brought home to this house. She took her first steps on this carpet. There are so many memories tied up in all of this brick and mortar."

"I know, but we'll always have those memories. You will always have us and, most of all, you will have *your* own house. I'll make sure of that, Mum, I promise! I promised nanna that I will always look after you and Hope and nothing can ever change that" Athena said earnestly.

"I know, love, but that will come in time. There is no rush. I'm glad we found a suitable house in the area we wanted. Watermead is a lovely estate and it has everything we want for now. I really thought we would end up somewhere awful," shuddered Hestia.

"Of course, we wouldn't end up somewhere awful," said Athena confidently. "As if I would let you stay somewhere awful. It might only be a rented accommodation, but it's an immaculate house and in a gorgeous estate like you said."

"I know, I'm not saying I didn't trust your choices or ability to find a house, but you can understand why I had to go with you to the south, to look for myself?"

"Of course, I understand. Anyway, I was glad you were there. The amount of houses to let was unbelievable. I can't believe we were actually lucky enough to get the house we did! It's perfect, isn't it, Mum?" enthused Athena.

"I agree. It's perfect! Well, it would be even better if it had three bedrooms."

"Oh, I don't mind sharing with Hope," Athena

rushed to assure her mum. "And Troy is moving in with Vickie.

I knew he would, it's about time too. You know what they say, Mum? New house, new baby!" teased Athena.

"Don't count on it. They are busy with other things. Work is very important to both of them. Just give them time and we'll see how things progress."

"Well, you never know," said Athena.

"Mum…mum…mum, the van's coming! Oh, look! It's huge!" screamed Hope with excitement.

"Okay, okay, calm down, young lady." shouted Hestia, over Hope's squeaks and giggles. "Stay out of the way of the removal men. We are all going to be very busy, so go sit on your chair by the front window and you will be able to see everything."

"Okay, but if you need any help, I'll be ready," Hope said proudly.

"Thank you, sweetie, but I think we'll manage," Hestia replied with a smile.

The next few hours flew past in a blur of activity, noise and quite a bit of confusion, but by 1 o'clock the house was empty of furniture and the men had gone for lunch. Apart from Hope, who was running from bedroom to bedroom, amazed by the new found space, there was no noise to be heard. Troy had left to take the last of his belongings to Vickie's house and Athena was due back any minute with Hamida, who wanted to say her good-byes in person.

Hestia walked slowly from the lounge through the dining room and kitchen and into her little square of Eden.

In this place, she would always find peace. Saying goodbye to her beautiful garden and having to walk away and leave her roses behind would be harder than saying goodbye to friends. And they say the English are eccentric!

But knowing she could not take them with her, she was sad and a little despaired. Doubts crowded in, trying to insinuate their way into her mind. Was she doing the right thing? Moving away, leaving her house. Giving up on her marriage. What about the children?

Feeling slightly panic stricken, she sat on her bench, breathed deeply the aroma of late summer roses, lavender, jasmine, gardenia and camellia mingled together. If only she could bottle that scent, she would walk away with a lighter heart. But, as it was, that voice came back, filtering like smoke from a neighbour's barbecue. *Your kids are already leaving you. Troy's moving out, Athena will be next and all you'll be left with is little Hope. Little ill Hope. No job, no house of your own. No way to get ahead. What will happen to Hope? You'll come back to me, you will come back running, asking me to forgive you. You need help Hestia, you are sick. You know you cant live without me. I cant wait.*

That's when Hestia realised that it was Zak's voice she was remembering that very last time they spoke. Only yesterday, but it seemed ages ago.

After the papers were signed and the keys handed over, they had left the office to go their separate ways. He had stopped her escape with a hand on her arm. Hestia knew he had to try again. He knew he could not cope without her, but there was no point. They both knew it, but he couldn't help himself, he had to ask..

"*It's not too late. We can try again. I made a*

mistake with that woman. I sent her back. There was only you! There will only be you!"

Hestia replied with a soft voice, *"Zak don't even try! You made a mistake? Going to Libya, marrying another woman, bringing her to England to live with you? That was not a mistake. But you know what was worse? You didn't do it to start again with someone, you could love and respect. You did it to spite me!"*

Zak looked Hestia in the eyes and said with a whine in his voice *"No I didn't! My family organised it all! After Mustafa told my sister, she arranged the meeting with Semira. When I met her, I was pressured into marriage. It was so complicated."*

Hestia replied, *"That's not an excuse Zak. You are not a child! You are old enough to know. You are a married man with three children. No one can force you to do anything you don't want to do. I know that better than anyone. You need help! Your temper is out of control and we both know that's because of the drugs!"*

What are you bloody talking about?" He thundered.

"Zak stop shouting!" Hestia said as she glanced

about the street. *"I've made excuses for years. Well that's the end of everything. You have got a drug problem. Just look at the mess you've made with your life. Look at you. No job, two wives, mistresses, temper, you constantly put the children down, hurt them, no wonder why they don't want to have anything to do with you. You hit them like there is no tomorrow, you verbally abuse them. Friends? You have hardly any. It's no good blaming everyone else. Look at the big picture, Zak. They can't all be wrong and you be the perfect one! I'm not trying to belittle you, Zak, but if you don't sit back and take a look at your life, how will you ever change it?"*

"Me change my life? Look at yours! Your kids are already leaving you. Troy's moved out, Athena will be next and all you will be left with is little Hope. Little ill Hope. No job, no house of your own. What will happen to Hope? You'll come back to me, you will come back running, asking me to forgive you. You need help Hestia, you are sick. You know you cant live without me. I cant wait. If you leave me Hestia you know I will come after you and I will not leave you alone. There is no way *you can ever start a new life. I will be watching your every move and your life will be made hell. Think about all this Hestia before you make a move. I will hunt you down and kill you and your kids.* He snarled arrogantly, so sure of his worth and her love for him that always made her back down.

"For your information, you cant scare me any more. Troy has moved in with his girlfriend, Vickie, and her little daughter, Amy. Athena and I will be taking Hope and moving into a beautiful house in a beautiful estate tomorrow. As for coming back, there is nothing here that I can't find anywhere else. Our life was based on a lie anyway Zak. Days in the sun where you told me that you were Italian, you were a Catholic and you told me our love would never die. There were moments in our lifetime that my heart still replays, there are moments I still love you the same way but then I remember the lies and deceits, the pain and the hurt and the abuse to the children that I cannot forgive and I know that life has to move on. Life has never seemed so promising. Goodbye Zak. I hope you do well in whatever you choose to do!"

Hestia turned round and strode down the street with her head held high and her back ramrod straight, ignoring all the foul words Zak flung at her retreating back.

The breeze caught that special scent, invading Hestia's thoughts like a balm on a burn. She was making preparations for a new life now. Athena had applied for the police force, two in fact, both within travelling distance from her new house. Troy had moved in with Vickie and Amy, starting his own family. Hope, well, Hope would need watching, but she was coping well. Yes, thought Hestia determinedly. Things were complicated, but she had a plan and so far that plan was unfolding nicely.

"Mum! Where are you?" came Athena's voice from the lounge.

"I'm coming," she replied, standing and returning from Eden.

"Hestia!" cried Hamida as she launched all 6'3' of herself, into Hestia's 5'5 frame. Hestia struggled a little.

"God, we are only going four hours down the

road!" said Athena grinning.

"I know, I know, but you try travelling four hours with all the boys!"

"Well, if you can make it, then we'll have you any time," replied Hestia graciously.

"Oh, thank you, Hestia," cried Hamida, weeping all over Hestia's reek.

"Oh, for goodness sake," Athena said.

"Oh, hush!" Both women said at the same time, then laughed.

"You will come, won't you?" begged Hestia.

"Of course, but it won't be easy with the boys," Assured Hamida.

"Well, you will always be welcome, whenever you can come. That looks like the removal men back from lunch," said Hestia sadly.

"Well, we'll drop you off on the way down."

"I brought the car. I knew the van was following you, so I knew it would be easier if I drove here. I suppose this is goodbye."

"Yes," said Hestia with a sniff.

"Oh God, you are both going to drown in a

minute," announced Athena, who had Hope on her back. "Come on, move it outside!"

"Okay, I can take a hint," said Hamida, smiling.

"I'll just lock up!" said Hestia.

"No, you won't! It's all done except for the front and back. I'll do that for you," decided Athena, taking the keys and pushing Hestia out the front door.

With a last hug, Hamida led the convoy out the cul-de-sac of and onto the motorway, A19. She parted company at the next junction with a beep and some frantic waving leaving only the Katti ladies, followed by huge van, to make their way four hours south to a new life and a brighter future. Hestia couldn't stop thanking the angels for making this happen. After so long she felt that she was finally free.

While they were driving, Zak's words played round Hestia's mind. She couldn't help but think to herself, was this the end, or was there more to come?

THE END?

190

191

www.ingramcontent.com/pod-product-compliance
Ingram Content Group UK Ltd.
Pitfield, Milton Keynes, MK11 3LW, UK
UKHW041438180426
11947UKWH00007B/502